EVERYTHING THAT GLITTERS AIN'T GOLD

AMBER MEEKS

SUPREME WORKS PUBLICATIONS

1

TAMMY

*C*hris & I sat in our living room, starring at each other in silence; neither one of us wanting to open up our mouth and say the wrong thing to each other. The tension in the room was so thick & heavy you could feel the elephant walking around the room. I honestly wanted to slap the shit out of him.

"So, are we going to talk about this or not? I'm not feeling the vibe between us right now," I said in a flat tone. I was tired of pussy footing around the situation. I wanted answers and I wanted them now!

"What do you want me to say T?" Chris replied in a defeated tone.

"ANYTHING to help me understand why you've been lying to me for the past six months Christopher," I said and watched as Chris cringed. He hated being called Christopher and I knew it. "Well if you're not going to say anything then I'm leaving. You called me to come home and talk and now you act like you can't open your mouth," I said grabbing my purse off of the coffee table and standing up. I took a step towards the door, but Chris jumped up from the couch and blocked my path.

"Baby don't leave without letting me explain. Whatever answers you need I'll give them to you," Chris said, almost begging. I looked at him and saw the sincerity in his eyes. I walked over to the love seat and sat down. Chris sat down next to me and took a deep breath. He reached for my hand and looked at my face, which was full of hurt and anger. I don't know why I was so upset, I just knew that I couldn't stand being lied to, no matter how small the lie was.

"Talk," I said in an angry but calm voice.

"Ok, well, remember around your birthday when I kept coming home early?" Chris said, and I nodded. "Well that's when I got fired babe. I wanted to tell you that same day, but I just couldn't. I've always been able to take care of you and I wasn't about to sit on my ass with no job while you're juggling school, work AND taking care of home. That's not my definition of a man. I'm sorry I lied to you T, but I promise it won't happen again. I love you. All I'm trying to do is provide for you," Chris said as he kissed me.

I kissed him back, but I couldn't shake the fact that my life would never be the same.

My boyfriend was now a drug dealer. Apparently, he got fired from his job six months ago and was now running the streets with his best friend, Kai'Juan. That would explain the nights that he's been coming home late, not answering is phone, etc. At first, I thought he was cheating until he finally came out and told me 45 minutes ago. I never wanted this life for Chris, and I constantly told him about his ghetto ass friend.

I'm not trying to be judgmental or anything, but Kai'Juan had some serious growing up to do and I always felt like he was a bad influence on my man. Chris wasn't that type of dude. He just wasn't about that life. Nothing good can come from this, and I don't know if I want to stick around and watch our lives crash and burn.

* * *

"So, he's a dope boy? Chris?" Anaya said as she started to laugh uncontrollably. Anaya was my older sister. My older, louder, more opinionated sister, which is saying something because I wasn't a timid female. I had no problem saying what was on my mind. Anaya, however, had absolutely no filter; she said whatever she wanted to say, when she wanted to say it and she didn't give a damn how you felt about it. Her loud demeanor was usually my favorite trait of hers, but right now I just wanted her to shut the fuck up. I looked at Anaya and rolled my eyes. Nothing was funny about this situation.

We were currently in the hotel suite I'd booked since finding out that Chris had this secret life he was hiding from me. I'd been here for about a week now and I desperately wanted to go home but I didn't know if I was ready to accept what he'd said to me.

I've known Chris since we were kids, we literally grew up together. We had our whole lives planned out and everything had been going according to plan. Becoming a drug king pin was NOT a part of the plan. Plus, that wasn't even like Chris to let Kai'Juan get him into some shit like this. He was a by the book dude. Even though he had that hood look to him, he was the opposite. On the outside, Chris reminded me of the actor Laz Alonso and even though he wasn't a punk by any means he just wasn't THAT dude. I know that I keep saying it, but it's true, or at least that's been my perception of him all these years.

"Tam, Chris ain't a hood nigga. I don't believe it. He's one of the good guys, he ain't tryna be like every other dude around here," Anaya said taking me away from my thoughts and becoming serious. She was currently in the mirror getting ready for a date with some guy she's met.

My sister was freaking gorgeous. Her skin was the color of peanut butter, and she was petite, yet curvy. We both looked damn near like twins, but I always felt like she was the "prettier sister". A lot of people said we resembled the singer Mila J, and I took that as a compliment. Our Mom was black and so was our dad, but his grand-mother was Asian which is where we get our chinky eyes and long hair from. My Mom, on the other hand, blessed us with the curves. I admired her for a few more seconds before responding to what she'd said to me.

"You think I don't know that? Chris has lost his damn mind and Kai'Juan is the reason, as usual. Any time Chris does some dumb shit Kai'Juan isn't too far behind," I told her, getting mad all over again.

"Damn for real?" Kai'Juan asked looking surprised. "How'd she take it?"

"I don't know. I think she took it ok but when she left she still looked mad," I said following Kai'Juan into the den/man cave and taking a seat on the leather couch. I grabbed the remote off the arm of the chair and turned on the huge flat screen that was mounted on the wall. I loved being in this room. It allowed me to have my space when Tammy or anybody else was working my nerves and allowed me to just be a man. I had a pool table (that I didn't use), a fully stocked bar and fridge, a big ass 60" TV and even a full bathroom in here. A nigga's paradise. I tried to convince Tammy to let me put a pole in here, but she wasn't having it.

"Get your mind off of her. Get out of this fucking house and let's go do something," Kai'Juan said, clearly annoyed by me. "Tammy ain't leaving you. After what y'all have been through over the years, this is like Christmas," Kai'Juan said suddenly going from annoyed to happy, laughing at his own statement. I, on the other hand just stared at him with a blank expression. Tammy being mad at me made me sick to my stomach. Literally.

"I know she won't leave, but I don't want her resenting me for doing what I gotta do to take care of us," I said and Kai'Juan shook his head.

"Nigga get out your feelings & come ride with me really quick," Kai'Juan said trying to get me out of the house. I thought about it for a second and then stood up. Fuck it, I might as well. I turned the TV off and then left the den for a moment, returning with my cellphone, car keys and wallet in my hands. Kai'Juan smiled, satisfied that I'd agreed to ride with him to wherever he planned to go.

"My nigga," he said to me as we headed out the door. We hopped in Kai'Juan's 2018 Escalade and pulled away from my house. A few minutes into the ride, Kai'Juan's phone rang.

"Who this?" Kai'Juan answered and I chuckled. You couldn't pay this nigga a billion dollars to say hello. He would always say, *"fuck I look like saying 'hello' to a nigga?"* I'd been friends with this nigga since diapers and I still wasn't used to his crazy antics. He definitely kept you on your toes. You never knew what to expect with him.

"BITCH I DON'T GIVE A FUCK! DUMB ASS!" Kai'Juan yelled into the phone. I looked at him and shook my head. *No chill, at all* I thought to myself. After listening to him going back and forth with whoever was on the phone, he hung up and tossed his phone in the cup holder. He was silent for a few moments before abruptly making a U-Turn in the middle of the road.

"Where the fuck are we going?" I asked.

"Look nigga, just shut the fuck up and ride. I need you with me in case I get the urge to slap the shit out of this bitch," Kai'Juan said angrily.

"Who?" I asked curiously.

"Janae dumb ass," Kai'Juan said. Janae was Kai'Juan's on again off again girlfriend. I know it's hard to believe this nigga had a girl, but the way he acted he might as well be single. I didn't like Janae for the simple fact that she let Kai'Juan fuck her over time after time. To me, she had no self-respect and because of that I didn't respect her.

After 10 minutes of driving, we pulled up to Janae's townhouse. She lived in a nice gated community, surrounded by the "upscale", successful black folk of Michigan. Even though Janae was stupid when it came to Kai'Juan, she was a very intelligent woman with a degree in business management. She just recently received her cosmetology license and was preparing to open up her "beauty lounge" as she liked to call it. She had everything going for herself which is why I couldn't understand why she wasted her time with my homeboy. Don't get me wrong, Kai'Juan was my nigga and blood couldn't make us any closer, but he was and probably always will be a dog. He said and did whatever he wanted, and he didn't give a fuck how anybody else felt about it. The man literally had no filter and you couldn't change him. He just wasn't built for this relationship. At least in my eyes he wasn't.

"This bitch just might die today," Kai'Juan said as he pulled his truck in the driveway behind Janae's 2017 cobalt blue Chevy Cruze.

The freshly manicured lawn was now covered with all of Kai'Juan's belongings.

Kai'Juan hopped out of his truck, damn near running toward the front door and I followed closely behind him. When we reached the porch, Janae was sitting on the steps with her phone in her hand and a blank expression on her face.

"You can quietly get your shit and go about your business," Janae said calmly.

"Bitch I ain't going no motherfucking where! You got me fucked up and yo ass gone get my shit off the motherfucking lawn and put it back where the fuck it's supposed to be! Stupid ass," Kai'Juan yelled while Jana just looked at him. "Nigga is you deaf? Speak when spoken to, rude ass," Kai'Juan said. See, that's the shit I'm talking about right there. He talked to her so crazy.

"Mothafucka, fuck you! Disrespectful ass, cheating ass, lying ass, stupid ass nigga! I'm so sick of you and your bullshit! Just get the fuck out of MY house!" Janae barked back at him. Kai'Juan paused for a moment before laughing.

"Why the fuck you putting emphasis on 'MY' house like I don't have my own shit? Ding dong dummy, I don't live with yo crazy ass and this is exactly why. Maybe if you stop listening to every bitch that you come across we'll be alright. I haven't fucked with no hoes in like a week," Kai'Juan said like that was a big accomplishment. This nigga was definitely out of his mind.

"Kai'Juan, we've been back together for the past 2 months," Janae said folding her arms and shifting her weight from her left side to the right. She was a really pretty dark-skinned girl with dimples, looking like Kelly Rowland just thicker. She could have any nigga she wanted, and she stuck with this fool. It was clear he didn't give a fuck about her.

"Oh," was all Kai'Juan said in response to her statement. "Well, shit, so? You know what type of nigga I am. Get my shit off the lawn Janae and start getting ready, I feel like going out tonight and you coming with me," Kai'Juan said before turning around and walking back towards his car. I stood there for a moment looking at Janae as the tears rolled down her cheeks. She shocked the hell out of me when she stood up and walked towards the lawn to start picking up Kai'Juan's belongings. I just shook my head and headed back to Kai'Juan's truck.

Once I was inside, Kai'Juan pulled off and headed in the direction of his dealership. Even though Kai'Juan was a hot head with no filter, he made smart decisions when it came down to his business and money. Yeah, he was a dope boy, but he was a boss, not just some corner boy. He was the king and he acted as if he owned the world. A ghetto king is what he called himself. Kai'Juan had enough bread to just chill but he said too much money wasn't enough. He opened a Ford dealership 3 years ago and it was doing extremely well. He was the only black dealer within 100 miles and I was proud of him for that. At the age of 25, Kai'Juan was really set for life, a young boss.

I wanted to say something about how he just handled Janae, but I wasn't about to waste my breath. Kai'Juan was gonna do whatever Kai'Juan wanted to do or say and nobody could change that but him. I'd tried so many times to get it through his thick ass skull that one day Janae was gonna realize she deserved better and really leave his ass, but he never listened. She'd been around for 5 years now and as many times as she'd threatened to leave, Kai'Juan never let her, so I guess she did mean something to him. He'd probably be sick if she ever walked away from him, but for now I'll just keep my mouth shut.

Pulling up to the dealership, I immediately spotted Kai'Juan's little brother Kannan working on a car in the auto shop.

"What up lil nigga?" I said to Kannan as I walked into the shop.

"What's good pussy?" Kannan spoke back. Kannan was 22 years old, in college working on his degree in sports medicine and working at the dealership to pay for tuition. He was the complete opposite of his brother, except for his player ways. I really didn't understand why niggas didn't appreciate the women in their lives. But then again, I was a different type of dude; at least I tried to be. Some women have even called me soft, but I was far from that. Kannan and I chatted for a while until this pretty brown skinned chick walked in to the shop. She was about 5'5" with pretty light brown eyes and cinnamon skin.

pretty cinnamon skinned woman, who smiled shyly at me once we made eye contact.

"Hello Ms. Sinclair, I'm Tasha Abraham," Tasha said shaking my hand.

"Hello Ms. Abraham, feel free to call me Tammy. I like to go on a first name basis with all my clients," I said offering a warm smile. I liked to refer to my patients as clients instead of patients. That way, it wouldn't make them feel uncomfortable or make them feel as if something was wrong with them.

"What brings you in today Tasha?" I asked ready to listen. I'd gotten my license in marriage/family counseling a year ago and I was loving every minute of it. I had my master's degree, but I was currently in school for my doctorate. I wanted to be Dr. Sinclair, not just Ms. Sinclair. I didn't like the sound of it.

Tasha went on to tell me her story and I listened intensely. I loved being a counselor. Hearing people's stories and giving them a different perspective, offering solutions to their conflicts made me happy. It was my passion in life and I couldn't imagine doing anything else.

After work, I headed straight home to start dinner. Yes, I've moved back home. I decided that nothing would be resolved if I was avoiding the issue by staying in the suite, so I came back home. I almost wish I would have just stayed in the suite because Chris was never here anyway.

"I can't get used to this," I said out loud to myself. I grabbed my cellphone, dialing Chris' number. He picked up on the third ring.

"Wassup bae?" Chris answered.

"Chris, where are you?" I asked.

"Out handling business with Juan. Wassup?"

"Just wondering where you were. I just got home from work. How long are you gonna be?"

"I'll be home in a couple of hours."

"Okay, I love you."

"Love you too bae," Chris said as he hung up.

I sat my phone down on the kitchen counter only to pick it right back up and dial my sister's number.

"Wassup TT?" Anaya said answering the phone.

"Nay I'm lonely. Chris is never here anymore. This shit is irritating," I complained.

"Aw hell naw, I don't wanna hear that whiny shit," Anaya said tired of me complaining. Ever since I found out about Chris linking up with Kai'Juan and being in the streets, I had become a complainer. I chose to stay so I just had to deal with it or walk away. At least that's what I keep telling myself.

"Nay for real. I've been having this bad feeling and then one of my patient's stories has me thinking," I said referring to Tasha and what she told me earlier. That girl had definitely been through a lot, very similar to me. When I was about 10 years old and Anaya was 12, our parents were killed in a car accident. After their death, we were sent to live with our grandmother on my Mom's side, Talia. We called her G TT (Grandma Talia). Because G TT raised me, we became very close. She was all I had besides Anaya to confide in. G TT made sure I knew that whatever a man brought to the table should be desert and not the main course. Because of her, I became the strong, independent woman that I am today.

When I was 18, I met a guy named Brandon, my first love. G TT knew from the first time she laid eyes on Brandon that he would break my heart. Of course, I didn't listen to her warning. For 3 years, I put up with Brandon and his cheating until I caught him with my former best friend, Imani. Ironically, Imani had been very vocal in her hatred for Brandon and vice versa. They were the last two people that I thought would betray me the way that they had. Shortly after I caught the two of them, Imani got pregnant and I finally just packed up and left him. You would think I would've left him as soon as I found out about the two of them, but I couldn't. Brandon had that much of a hold over me; but him getting Imani pregnant was enough for me to leave. I thank God that I did. To this day, Brandon will pop up out of the blue trying to inch his way back in my heart, but I would never allow myself to be broken hearted again.

"Girl I know you hear me talking to you!" Anaya screamed into the phone.

"My bad Nay, I was thinking," I said staring out the kitchen window.

"About what?" she asked.

"Brandon," I admitted.

"Girl bye! First, you're mad because Chris is in the streets to take care of yo yellow ass, and now you are thinking about Satan himself? Get off my phone with your foolishness," she said before hanging up on me. I rolled my eyes, placed my phone on the counter and walked over to the kitchen to get some meat out to make for dinner. What was the point of having this gorgeous house if I was going to be in it alone?

While preparing dinner, I couldn't get my mind off both Tasha and Brandon. *Get it together Tam* I said to myself and continued cooking. I kept reminding myself that I was cooking for a man I know would never do me the way Brandon did. I was stupid for even letting him come across my mind.

4

KAI'JUAN

"All the money needs to be moved from here over to the house on Patton and then burn this bitch down," I said to one of my workers. I'd been at the stash house all day doing an inspection and making sure my workers followed "moving day" protocol. I liked to switch up the stash houses every month just to be on the safe side. That way, if money was ever off I knew exactly who was responsible. I'd called Chris 30 minutes ago to pick me up so that we could attend our first meeting with our new connect. As I was wrapping up my instructions, Chris called to let me know he was outside.

"By 3:30 I expect a phone call saying that everything went smoothly," I said to G, who was one of my workers. I'd made him the "head of operations" because I knew he was solid and that the niggas I had working under him respected him enough to not fuck up. He reported directly to me and notified me of any updates, good or bad. I trusted him to a certain extent, but I still had eyes everywhere. If there were any snakes in my grass it wouldn't take long for me to figure it out and I didn't have a problem eliminating any problems.

"Got you boss," G said as he went down to the basement to collect the safe and start the process of moving the work, weapons and money to its new location.

One night, while Chris and Tammy were out having dinner. Brandon texted Tammy letting her know she needed to tell Chris about them or he would do it his self later that night. As soon as Tammy was about to open her mouth and explain everything, Chris blurted out that he loved her. Once those words came out of his mouth, it was a wrap for Brandon. That same night Tammy told B that she chose Chris and he seemed to just disappear off the face of the earth. Obviously, Tammy has a golden pussy or something because she had both of my niggas going crazy over her, and it seems as if she still does.

About a year after Brandon disappeared, he resurfaced and was back on his quest to win Tammy. He began texting and calling her phone at all times of the day and night, disrespecting Chris, doing whatever he thought it would take to win back his first love. Finally, Tammy came clean with Chris, telling him how torn she was when they first started dating and how she considered going back to Brandon until Chris admitted that he loved her. No surprise that Chris didn't get upset with Tammy. He was more pissed off with Brandon because he felt that his "friend" should have let it be known that Tammy was the girl that "got away" in a sense. From then on, Chris has been holding a dumb ass grudge that he's probably never gonna get over.

After Brandon & I finished handling business, I headed back to the truck, ready to listen to whiny ass Chris. He was my nigga and everything, but I was so tired of hearing him complain. He was either in this shit or he was out. All that emotional shit all the time was going to kill my business and I couldn't have that. After listening to fifteen minutes of "fuck that hoe ass nigga, he ain't never getting my girl," I had heard enough.

"Nigga shut the fuck up! Damn! Everybody knows how you feel about T and more importantly how she feels about you! I'm tired of hearing you whine and complain. That emotional shit makes me wanna break yo jaw just, so you can shut the fuck up! Look, I know you love your girl and what not, but I can't hear this every day. What you need to do is boss the fuck up. Decide if you want to be in this shit or out. If you want to be in that's cool, but if you don't that's cool too. I know you not really cut like that. I can set you up with a position at the dealership. I know you want to be a man and take care of home and that's dope C but make a decision. And if you choose to be in this game, you gotta stop letting niggas see that soft side of you. Niggas look at that as a weakness and I can't have no weak niggas on my team. And another thing, if you gone be in you gotta learn how to put that petty bullshit with B to the side. Once upon a time before Tammy pussy whipped y'all we used to be brothers. Fuck that, we still brothers and I need y'all goofy asses to get it together," I preached. Chris looked at me and was about to respond but stopped when he heard my phone ring.

"Wassup baby?" I said into the phone. "Yeah I'm about to have C drop me off at yo shit. Be naked, I need some pussy," I said smirking. I hung up the phone and glanced over at Chris who was shaking his head. "What?" I asked playing dumb.

"Janae is a dumb ass. You talk to her so crazy," Chris said.

"She ain't stupid. She knows her fucking place and she knows she ain't going nowhere. I'll kill her," I said seriously.

"Now when she finds somebody to treat her right you'll be looking stupid," Chis said.

"I do treat her right. She gets this dick every night. I'm always under her ass when I'm not taking care of business. These other hoes just there. She the only one that matters. Bitch you know that. Don't try to make me an emotional ass nigga like you," I said as I pulled up to Janae's house. I got out and headed into the house and up the stairs to Janae's bedroom. When I got there, I found her in the bathroom.

"Man you don't listen! Why aren't you naked Janae?" I yelled. I sat on the bed and blew out a frustrated breath. This girl never follows directions. Janae came out of the bathroom a few minutes later, fully clothed, which pissed me off. I looked at her and sucked my teeth.

"You really got me fucked up. You think I'm going to do whatever you tell me? Last time I checked my Daddy's name was Antonio Evans not Kai'Juan James," Janae said with an attitude. She was dressed in some jogging pants and a white wife beater. Her brown hair was pulled back into a ponytail and no make-up was on her face. She reminded me of Kelly Rowland with smooth brown skin, big eyes and curly hair. She was beautiful to me, and even more beautiful standing here yelling at me.

"You're right baby. I'm sorry for talking to you crazy. I just don't know how else to talk to motha...I mean people," I said, catching myself from cussing.

"Yes you do, you just choose to talk to everybody like you own them. I'm not one of those people. That shit ain't cute," Janae said rolling her eyes and walking out of the room. She wasn't buying my bullshit. She knew I would say anything when I wanted some pussy, and right now, I wanted some bad. I let out a groan as I walked out of the room right after her. I thought about chasing after her but quickly changed my mind and walked right down the stairs and out of the door. As soon as I was outside, I pulled my phone out, scrolled through my contacts and stopped when I saw Lauren's name. Lauren was the main chick I fucked with when Janae was on my nerves, which was damn near all the time.

"Wassup Ky?" Lauren spoke into the phone.

"What up doe?"

"You need me?"

"You already know."

"Say less. Come on," Lauren said and then disconnected the call. I put my phone in the cup holder of my car and smirked. *Why the fuck can't Janae be that simple?* I thought to myself and then headed in the direction of Lauren's crib to get my mind right.

5

TAMMY

"You know what Chris? You really on my damn nerves with this shit," I said to Chris. It was Friday night and we had plans to go out to dinner and spend some quality time, but he's canceled on me...again.

"Baby I know you're mad but we gotta go get this money," Chris said. I was tired of hearing that bullshit. Just two months ago he was acting all scared like he really didn't wanna be in the streets and now he was acting like he loved the shit.

"I don't even have the strength to argue with you. Just go," I said, disappointed. I hated that we never spent any time together. He went to kiss me, but I turned my head and he ended up kissing my cheek.

"Look baby, I love you, you know that. I'm doing what I gotta do so we can be good. You gotta understand that," he said to me. Before I could respond, his phone started ringing. After a few *yeah's,* Chris told who I assume is Kai'Juan that he was on his way.

"You got me fucked up Chris. For real. Kai'Juan don't even need you for real. I need you!" Tammy pouted.

"T, chill the fuck out," Chris said, grabbing his keys off the counter. "I'll be back later," he said and was out of the door. I sat on

6

BRANDON

*S*he still wants a real nigga, I knew she did. I'm definitely getting my baby back. Chris don't know what to do with that, ole weak ass nigga. I walked back over to the VIP section, joining Kai'Juan.

"Nigga, I ain't about to get in the middle of you & C's business, but you need to stay the fuck away from T. She ain't yours no more. Leave it the fuck alone before I have to shoot yo ass for being stupid," Kai'Juan said throwing back a shot of patron.

"Bitch I wish you would," Brandon said laughing. We continued to crack jokes and observe the females dancing and having a good time. Multiple bitches came up to me flirting and trying to dance on me, but I wasn't even feeling it. Although it was some bad ass bitches in this club, they weren't T. I need that girl. I watched her like a hawk for the rest of the night, dancing, drinking and having a good time with her girls. She seemed happy at the moment, but I knew better. Something was up, and I was going to find out sooner or later.

KAI'JUAN

*E*ither this bitch is stupid, or she just didn't give a fuck. I know her ass see me in this club. She was drinking and shaking her ass like she didn't have a man, with her little thot ass. I glanced around the club and saw a couple of females I fucked with from time to time. If Janae wanted to play it crazy, then we could definitely play it crazy. I smiled when I saw Lauren walk into the club looking good as fuck in an all-black body suit. Her titties were sitting up just right and her ass was looking fatter than usual. I made up my mind in 0.5 seconds that I was hitting that after the club. Lauren spotted me and made her way to my section. Once she approached me, she wrapped her arms around me before whispering that she wanted me in my ear.

"My thoughts exactly," I told her, grabbing her ass. She giggled and then turned around and started twerking on me once the DJ played *Booty* by Blac Youngsta. After a few seconds, my dick got hard. I looked around the club to see if I could find Janae. I found her staring at me with a deadly look on her face. I smirked, blew a kiss at her and then winked. She continued to give me the death stare before making her way to the steps, and I knew she was headed my way. One thing about my baby, it wasn't no hoe in her blood. She didn't play about her man. On the flip side, Lauren didn't have a problem showing her ass either, and I wasn't about to stop shit unless I needed to. Janae made her way over to me and forcefully grabbed Lauren by her arm, sending her falling to the floor.

"Get the fuck off my nigga hoe!" Janae screamed, ready to beat Lauren's ass. Lauren got up off the floor, looked at her and laughed.

"He might be your nigga, but that's definitely my dick. I'll see you later Kai'Juan," Lauren said grabbing her drink that was behind me on a table and walking off, joining her girls.

"So, you fucking that bitch?" Janae asked, getting in my face.

"Only when you playin' it crazy," I said, honestly. I'm not the type of nigga to lie. You were either gonna deal with me or you weren't. *SLAP!* Immediately, my cheek started to sting. This bitch really put her hands on me.

"You a dirty motherfucka! I hope your dick falls off! You better pray to God I don't have nothing!" Janae said. She tried to walk away but I grabbed her arm.

"Put your fucking hands on me again and I'm beating yo ass. Take yo silly ass home, I'll be there in a minute. We need to have a talk," I told her. She snatched her arm away from me and walked off, while I went back to the couch in the VIP section and ordered another drink. *She better have her ass at home*, I thought.

"Nigga she gone kill you" Brandon said, laughing.

"She ain't gon do shit but what the fuck I just said," I said taking my drink from the waitress. I wasn't to be fucked with and Janae knew that. I'd deal with her when I got home, but for now, I was going to chill with my dog.

CHRIS

𝒦ai'Juan asked me to come out to Flame with him, but the club wasn't my thing. I decided to just go on home and chill with my girl, but that idea went out the window when I pulled in the driveway and noticed she wasn't at home. It seemed like her ass stayed mad at me, but she'll be alright When she got home I was gonna tell her to pack a bag because I was taking her to Chicago for the weekend. Earlier, I booked us a suite at this hotel named Sybaris. Tammy had been talking about it for a while, so I knew she'd be excited to go. The suites were out cold, equipped with a Jacuzzi and a pool inside the room. The suite I booked had a waterfall feature above the pool, real romantic and shit. She couldn't be mad at that. I texted Tammy asking her where she was and what time she was coming home before hopping in the shower. Once I got out the shower, I changed into some basketball shorts and socks and chilled on the bed, watching TV. About two hours had passed before I realized that Tammy still hadn't texted back. I looked at the clock and noticed it was 2:47 am. I texted Tammy again and called her 3 times, back to back, but still received no answer. At this point, I was starting to get annoyed. She couldn't be that mad at me.

Finally, damn near an hour later, I heard Tammy come through

"No, you chill the fuck out!"

"Why you trippin?" Kai'Juan said sitting on the bed and kicking his shoes off. I wanted to punch him right in his throat. He looked at me and licked his lips again. He was so sexy to me when he did that. Listen to me, my weak ass.

"Come here baby," he said to me. I slowly walked over to him and sat beside him. He got up, standing in front of me and then leaned down to kiss me.

"I hate yo Drake looking ass so much. Why do you do me so dirty Kai?" I asked as I broke away from the kiss. Kai'Juan looked at me for a second before smirking.

"I love you too baby," he said kneeling down on his knees and pulling me to the edge of the bed. He pulled my panties off and I already knew what was about to go down. As soon as I felt that magical tongue of his, all was forgotten.

We made love for a few hours and then fell asleep. My sleep, however, was cut short by Kai'Juan's phone ringing.

"Kai get your phone," I said groggily.

"You get it," he replied. I let out a frustrated breath and reached my hand out to feel around for the ringing phone. I opened one eye to see what time it was but was quickly awakened when I saw a picture of the hoe that was twerking on my man last night. The ringing ceased, and I sat up in the bed. As soon as my back touched the headboard, the ringing started again, and I quickly answered.

"Hello?" I said with an attitude.

"Oh hey wifey," the bitch said on the other end. "Can you tell our nigga to wake up? He's supposed to take me to work today," she said in a calm town. I looked at the phone and then at Kai'Juan. This motherfucker had me so fucked up.

"Kai," I said as calm as I possibly could.

"Yeah baby?" he answered sleepily.

"Your bitch is on the phone," I said.

"Who?" Kai'Juan asked sitting up. I looked at the phone again to see her name.

"Lauren," I said. Kai'Juan scrunched his face in an irritated fashion.

"Hand me the phone," he said with his hand out and I looked at him like he had lost his damn mind. Instead of handing him the phone I put it back up to my ear.

"Bitch call an Uber," I said into the phone and then threw it against the wall.

"Dog what the fuck!" Kai'Juan shouted.

"Get out and don't come back. I'm done Kai'Juan. You keep proving to me that you don't give a fuck about me and I keep trying to make you love me. You don't deserve me, and I deserve better than your disrespectful ass," I said calmly. I was kind of scaring myself. I've never been so mad that I was calm. I felt like I could take this man's life at any minute.

"Man, it's too early Nae. We can talk when we get up," he said trying to pull me back in the bed. I snatched away from him and hopped out of the bed.

"I'm dead ass serious. I'm tired of this back and forth. I'm a damn good woman that deserves a man who will treat me right. Clearly, that man isn't you. I'm done with you," I said to him. He looked me dead in my eyes and I could see the look of shock on his face.

"So you don't love me?" he asked.

"It's not about love. I've loved you since we were 18 and you still can't get it right. You don't want or need a relationship and I don't need you," I said. I don't know what it was but with every word that I spoke, it felt like a weight was being lifted off of my shoulders. We sat there in my bedroom, silent for several minutes before Kai'Juan got up and started to put his clothes on.

"Regardless of everything Nae, I did and do love the fuck out of you. You mean more to me than any of these hoes, and you're right, maybe I don't need a relationship. I'll give you the break and space that you want, but we fasho ain't done," he said before walking out of the room. A couple of seconds later, I heard the front door close. Everything he said to me went in one ear and out of the other. He didn't mean none of that shit and I was done falling for it.

CHRIS

Two Weeks Later

Our trip to Chicago definitely did us some good. We were getting back on track and Tammy seemed to be happier than I had seen her in a long time. As long as she was good, I was good.

I'd been working with Kai'Juan for 7 months now and I had stacked enough bread for me and T to be straight for a while. I was on my way to Kai'Juan's dealership to talk business. He knew I wasn't tryna be in the streets like him and he said he had an idea for me. Whatever it was, I trusted my boy and his judgement. When I pulled up I saw Brandon and some girl leaning against Brandon's Challenger, talking. I was going to park in the front, but after seeing this nigga, I went around back. I wasn't about to let him get under my skin, not today.

Once I got to the back, I knocked on Kai'Juan's office door. After I heard him say come in, I turned the knob and entered the spacious office. If nothing else, my nigga had taste. The office wasn't too flashy, but it was modern, and it gave off a vibe that was very professional yet comforting at the same time. In my opinion, his personality wasn't the least bit comforting, but I knew he meant well deep down inside.

Kai'Juan was sitting at his desk with a blank expression on his face, seemingly in deep thought.

"Bro you good?" I asked him.

"Man hell naw," he said looking up at me.

"What's the problem?" I asked with concern. The way he was looking off into space made me a little nervous, so I sat down in the chair on the other side of his desk.

"Janae really ain't fucking with me. It's been two weeks bro. She ain't never went this long without talking to me. I haven't seen her or nothing. I'm starting to think it's another nigga. On everything I love I swear I'll kill his ass," he ranted. I told his ass that his day was gonna come but he never wanted to listen. He thought that he could do whatever he wanted, and it wouldn't be any consequences.

"Nigga I told you this shit was gonna happen. Now look at you, in here moping around like a little ass girl. I don't feel sorry for you at all. It's about time she left you. You did her dirty for years and you thought it wasn't gonna be any consequences? Why do you expect for her to keep taking you back? A person can only take so much," I said to him. I wasn't about to sugarcoat shit for this nigga. It's time that he woke the fuck up and realized that his actions were causing him to lose people he loved. He couldn't be hard with everybody, especially not his woman.

"Man fuck you. I'm done speaking on it. Let's talk business," he said completely ignoring everything I just said to him. Fuck it, he wasn't going to listen and that wasn't my problem. He went on to tell me that he had a need for a general manager at the dealership and he thought that I'd be a good fit. I was happy that he'd offered me a position, but I knew that it would feel weird working for him when I was so used to working with him.

"I don't know about working for you," I said honestly.

"Come on now C, you know it won't even be like that," he said leaning back in his chair and checking his phone.

"I don't know. I'll think about it and let you know by Friday," I said.

"Alright, bet," he said dapping me up.

"And get out your feelings mothafucka," I said laughing.

"Bitch you the softest nigga on the planet. I don't wanna hear that shit," Kai'Juan said. I just laughed and walked out of his office. On my way to my car, I spotted that cinnamon skinned girl I'd seen before, looking around. She must have felt me staring because she looked up, smiled and waved at me. I did the same. She motioned for me to come over to her, so I did.

"Do you work here?" she asked. I laughed a bit.

"No not yet, but I will be starting next week. How can I help you?" I asked her.

"Well, I was looking to buy a new car but nobody in here has asked me if I needed help," she said.

"Well you're in luck. I'm good friends with the owner. Would you like for me to go and get him?" I asked her.

"Yes, please," she said politely. I headed back to Kai'Juan's office and walked in, quickly wishing I had knocked first. Angela, the receptionist, was on her knees giving Kai'Juan head, and he seemed to only be partially into it. Angela was an okay looking girl. She wasn't ugly, but she wasn't fine either, just average. She even had an average body, but that let me know that just like every other female, Kai'Juan didn't give a fuck about her. When she heard the door open, she quickly got up, trying to get herself together. Kai'Juan, on the other hand didn't seem fazed by me entering the room.

"The fuck you stop for?" he asked Angela with his face contorted into an irritated expression. She gave him a look like she was disgusted.

"Nigga, that's why," she said with attitude, pointing at me.

"Man keep going. C ain't nobody," he said to her. Angela looked hesitant at first, but then got back down on her knees and started sucking like her life depended on it. I just shook my head. Kai'Juan was my nigga and all but that nigga was stupid as fuck. I couldn't change the nigga though, he was a grown ass man that was going to do whatever the fuck he wanted to do. I guess that's why he got along so well with Brandon, the niggas acted just alike.

11

TAMMY

*E*verything was going so well at the moment. Work was steady, school was about to start soon, and Chris and I were good again. On the outside everything seemed perfect, but he'd be pissed if he knew I'd been texting Brandon since that night at the club. I don't know what it was, but he'd been like my diary, just like old times before we became a couple. I wasn't cheating on Chris or anything like that, Brandon was just someone that I felt comfortable talking to and he knew me. I still felt bad about it though. If Chris ever found out, I know it would break his heart.

"What you over there thinking about so hard?" Chris asked, pulling me away from my thoughts.

"I'm sorry babe. I'm just thinking about a lot," I said, keeping my response short and simple.

"You wanna talk about it?" he asked.

"No, I'm good. Thanks for asking though," I said cuddling up next to him. We were sitting on the couch with a big bowl of popcorn, watching Netflix. I loved chill days like this, just spending quality time. There was no better feeling to me. I pulled myself from my own thoughts & concentrated on my man and the movie we were watching.

About 30 minutes later, just as I was getting into the movie, my phone vibrated. I ignored it until it vibrated two more times. Finally, I grabbed the phone off of the coffee table in front of me and looked at the phone. I saw that I had 3 text from Brandon. I wasn't going to respond, but curiosity got the best of me.

B: T wyd?

B: I'm bored as fuck!

B: Let's do something today

I read the messages and laughed inwardly.

Me: Lol. Chillin w/ my man right now

B: How about later? You can't be chillin that hard if you're texting me.

Me: Whatever B

B: Meet me at Dave & Buster's tonight. I wanna have some fun with you

Me: Ok

Lord, please help me. I knew what I was doing was probably wrong, but I liked the friendship that Brandon and I had. I just hoped that when it came to light, Chris would be understanding, but that was wishful thinking.

12

KAI'JUAN

I missed Janae like a mothafucka. She was really done, and it was messing with me real bad. It's like a piece of me is missing. She got me sounding like a straight bitch. I gotta think of a way to get my girl back.

"Kai you aren't even listening," Lauren said, interrupting my thoughts. I looked over at her and instantly got irritated. This bitch was starting to become annoying.

"Naw I wasn't," I said nonchalantly. She sucked her teeth and rolled her eyes. "I really don't give a fuck about your attitude," I said to her, getting up from the bed and grabbing my clothes.

"Where the fuck you going at 4am Kai'Juan?" she questioned me. I looked at her like she had grown two heads. She had me fucked up.

"Bitch you're not my girl. Don't question me about shit!" I let her know. This bitch really lost her mind. I started spending a little more time with her when Janae left, but she was getting a little too carried away now.

"Oh, so all of a sudden I'm not your girl? You said if you & Janae don't work out that we'd be together," she said looking hurt. I almost felt bad, but I snapped out of it. I didn't really give a fuck about her feelings.

"I said that shit because I wanted some pussy, not because I meant it. Janae could call me right now and say she wants me back and I promise you'll never see or hear from me again," I said honestly.

"Wow, really? You ain't shit!" she said folding her arms and leaning back on the bad with a full-blown attitude.

"I don't give a fuck! You know I ain't shit but yet yo dumb ass still fuckin with me. Man, you know what? I'm good on you," I said and walked out of the door. I wasn't about to deal with her stupid ass at all. As soon as I got in my car, she started blowing my phone up, but I ignored it. During the 15-minute drive to my house I ignored 65 calls and 15 text messages from Lauren. Once I realized she wasn't going to stop calling, I answered.

"WHAT?" I yelled into the phone. "I told you I'm good on you and I meant that shit. Stop calling my fucking phone, crazy ass bitch!" I said.

"Well hello to you too," Janae's voice said through the phone, catching me totally off guard.

"Damn Nae, my bad. I thought you were somebody else".

"Clearly," Janae chuckled.

"Wassup man? I miss you," I admitted. I was acting like such a pussy, but I didn't care.

"You should. I was calling because I wanted to know if you would ride down to Atlanta with me. I'm going to my family reunion and I'm not ready to tell anybody we aren't together anymore," Janae said. I smiled, but my smile quickly went away.

"Why are you lying to your people though?" I asked her. I don't get why she didn't want her family to know. Shit, she's the one that left me, it wasn't the other way around.

"Because they love you and I don't feel like explaining why you're not there," she said sounding sad. I instantly felt fucked up. I had to find a way to make this right between us.

"I'll go. I'll do anything for you," I said.

"Thanks Kai. I appreciate it. We leave on Saturday. I'll text you the flight information."

"Yo, Nae, I don't wanna fly. How about we drive? I want to spend some time with you."

"I don't know. I'll think about it and let you know," she said and then hung up abruptly. I looked at the phone and smirked. I had to get a plan in motion real quick. We might be leaving the city broken up, but we were fasho coming back as a couple.

"Thank you. I'm good. It seems like I'm always up here," she giggled.

"Yeah, I noticed. You know somebody that works up here?" I asked.

"Yeah, my brother Hakeem," she said as she shifted her weight from one leg to the other.

"Oh, damn, Keem is your brother? That's my nigga with his silly ass," I chuckled.

"Yeah, he is goofy. Always calling me up here for nothing," she playfully rolled her eyes and then glanced around the dealership.

"Well, I'm glad that he does. I don't mean to sound too forward, but would you mind if I call you some time? We keep bumping into each other, I figure it has to be for a reason," I said sincerely, shoving my hands in my pockets. She smiled again, showing her perfectly white teeth.

"That's sweet of you. I can always use a handsome new friend," she said, stressing the word friend. I chuckled again. "Let me see your phone," she said holding her hand out for my phone. I dug in my pocket to retrieve my phone, unlocked it and then handed it to her. She plugged her number in and then handed it back to me.

"Make sure you call me. I'm sorry, what was your name again?" she asked.

"Chris," I stated.

"Right, Chris. Make sure you call me," she said again, this time a little more flirtatious.

"Oh I definitely will," I said walking away. I was probably wrong as fuck for doing that, but shit if Tammy wanted to be sneaky I could too. Two can play this game.

Later that night, when I got home, I found Tammy in the living room, on the couch, staring at the TV. The only thing that caused me to be a little worried was that the TV wasn't on.

"What's wrong T?" I asked, concerned. I walked over to the couch and sat next to her. She looked depressed and stressed the fuck out and I didn't know why. I pulled her close to me, putting her head on my chest. As soon as her head hit my chest, she burst out in tears.

"Baby you're scaring me. Tell me what's wrong," I said, trying to comfort her but also wanting answers.

"Chris..I'm...I'm pregnant!"

TAMMY

I'm pregnant. With a whole baby. A whole fucking little human. What am I supposed to do with a baby?

"You're really pregnant? Baby, that's amazing!" Chris said excitedly, lifting me up in the air.

"We can't keep it," I said. I had to catch myself since this nigga almost dropped my ass on the floor.

"The fuck you mean?" he asked angrily. In this moment, he looked like he wanted to kill me.

"We're not ready Chris and you know it."

"Fuck that! We about to get ready. Fuck is wrong with you bro?" he yelled. At that point, I couldn't control it and the tears just started pouring out. "What the fuck Tammy? Are you sure it's even mine?" he asked, and I slapped the shit out of him.

"Fuck you. Don't ask me no shit like that!" I yelled.

"Well, shit, you never know. The way you been on Brandon's dick lately," he said. As soon as the words left his mouth it was like all the air had been sucked out of my body. "What? You silent now? You think I didn't know? You foul Tammy. You foul as fuck. That's who you want? Huh? Go be with that dirty mothafucka then!" he yelled, pacing back and forth. I don't think I've ever seen him this angry, especially at me.

"Baby, I'm sorry ok? I don't want him baby, I swear. He's just easy to talk to, I promise," I said sobbing. This couldn't be happening right now.

"Man fuck that Tammy. Ain't no bitch about to be sneaking and talking to no nigga she's just cool with. Man, fuck this, I'm out," Chris said as he snatched his keys off of the couch and walked out of the door, slamming it in the process. I just sat there crying my eyes out. I had never been so upset and confused. After 25 minutes of crying, I got myself together and called my sister.

"T Money what's the deal!" Anaya said excitedly.

"Hey Nay," I said, sniffling.

"Why you sound sad boo? What's wrong?" she asked. Immediately, I started to explain everything to her. When I finished, Anaya had nothing to say, and if Anaya was speechless, I knew I fucked up.

"Well, is the baby Brandon's sis?" she asked.

"No! Hell no Nay! I mean, me and B have been kicking it, but we haven't kissed, touched, fucked, nothing. We're just friends. Period," I said to her.

"Well your friend is about to cost you a good man," Anaya said, and I knew she was telling the truth. "Wait a damn minute, do you still want Brandon bitch?" Anaya asked. I sighed before I responded.

"I really don't know Nay," I admitted.

"Bitch, good night!" she said and hung up before I could say another word. I felt so bad. Chris was so good to me, but sometimes I felt he was just too soft. Then again, I knew Brandon would just break my heart again. I couldn't help the fact that a piece of my heart was still with him. He was like my best friend.

My phone vibrated next to me and I looked down at the caller ID. Brandon's name popped up and I smiled subconsciously.

"Wassup B?"

"T-Dub, what up doe?" Brandon asked.

"Nothing much. What you up to?"

"Shit, chillin. Where you at? I'mma come scoop".

"I'm at home."

"Bet. I'm right over here on Outer Drive and 6 mile. Be ready in 10 minutes," he said before we hung up. Thankful for the distraction, I got up and went to the bathroom to wash my face before he pulled up.

About 30 minutes later, Brandon and I pulled up at Metro Beach. I looked at him and punched him in the arm.

"Nigga! What you trying to do, rekindle a romance? I asked giggling.

"Oh so you remember, huh?"

"Of course I do. This was our first date. Actually, my first date ever," I said reminiscing.

"Man, you were so nervous," he said laughing at his own thoughts. I laughed as well.

"Of course I was nervous! I didn't know what to do with a nigga that fine," I said but quickly regretted saying it.

"Oh, so you think I'm still fine?" he asked, licking his lips like LL Cool J.

"Boy, bye," I said playfully, tucking a piece of hair behind my ear. We ended up stopping in the middle of the beach and Brandon laid down a towel so that we could sit down. We sat there for a few moments, in silence, just lost in our own thoughts.

"Yeah, you do. I miss you though T. I never apologized for that shit with Imani. I was young and dumb as fuck. I fucked up the best thing that ever happened to me. I mean, you were my best friend and I'm really sorry that I hurt you," he said sincerely. I knew he was sincere just by looking in his eyes. Old feelings started to come back, and I felt like I was a teenager all over again. To say I was scared was an understatement. I shouldn't be feeling like this with anyone who isn't Chris...oh shit, Chris! I couldn't do this. Not to him.

"Brandon, I can't do this," I said. He looked at me funny.

"What you mean? We ain't doing nothing but talking," he said.

"Yeah but we are reminiscing. That ain't gone lead to nothing but trouble," I told him. Brandon scrunched up his face, looking at me.

"You really don't trust yourself around me? You've known me for how many years and you say some stupid shit like that?" he asked.

"That's exactly why I don't trust myself because I know you and I know me. I can't do that to Chris. He's too good of a man to me," I said to him, honestly. As soon as I mentioned Chris' name his whole attitude changed.

"Alright," was all he said as he started up his car and pulled off. It was so like him to get an attitude as soon as something wasn't going his way. He acts real hard but deep down he's a big ass baby. Once we got to my house, I turned in my seat to look at him.

"B, you know I love you and you're one of my best friends, but I also know how you and Chris feel about each other and it's just not right for us to keep this friendship going knowing my man hates your guts. I just can't. I feel like I'm cheating," I said. Brandon was silent for several minutes before he licked his lips then turned to look at me.

"Alright T, I can't do nothing but accept how you feel. This is your decision. But you know I'll always be here," he said and then shocked the hell out of me by leaning towards me and giving me one of the most passionate kisses I'd ever experienced. The kiss lasted for what felt like a good 5 minutes before I broke away. Instantly tears formed in my eyes. I grabbed my purse from the back seat and hopped out the car all in one quick motion.

"What the fuck!" I said to myself. I needed to get myself together and I needed to do it quickly before I ruined everything.

JANAE

I know I said I wanted Kai'Juan to go with me on this trip but damn! I didn't know it was gonna be this hard! He was looking good as fuck on purpose and it was pissing me off.

"What you over there thinking about girl?" Kai'Juan said taking his attention off the road for a moment to look at me. We were riding in his Escalade heading towards my family reunion in Atlanta and all I could do was think about us. I hate that he had to fuck us up

"Nothing," I lied.

"Yo ass lying," he said.

"You don't know my life," I said smiling at him.

"Awww shit, I got you to smile? Nae feeling the kid again," he said cockily. I laughed.

"Ain't nobody thinking about you Kai."

"Yo, you a fucking liar, but its ok, I love you too baby," he said grabbing my thigh and squeezing it. I was tempted to tell him to pull over, but I kept my composure. How in the hell was I about to survive this family reunion, pretending that I'm with him, when I can barely control myself in the car? I grabbed my purse and dug around for my iPhone and headphones and turned on some music. I couldn't talk to Kai'Juan right now without getting in my feelings.

Five or six hours later, I told Kai'Juan to just get a room for the night because I was exhausted, and I knew he was too. "But you ain't feeling me though. Liar," Kai'Juan said laughing and getting out the car to go pay for the room. What the fuck was I thinking? I'm setting myself up for failure. But shit, I'm tired. A couple minutes later, Kai'Juan came back to the car and grabbed our bags then led the way to the room. Once in the room, I frowned. The hotel room was average, and I was expecting that. What I wasn't expecting was the one king size bed in the middle of the room.

"Why the fuck did your stupid ass get one bed?" I yelled angrily.

"Man chill the fuck out. I don't give a fuck if we not together, you love me, and I love you. Eventually, we'll be back together, and you know it. Stop acting like you don't know me and shut the fuck up and go to bed. Shit," Kai'Juan said before walking away and going into the bathroom.

That's exactly the type of shit I hated, his slick ass mouth. I couldn't front though, it kind of turned me on. I heard the shower running, so I decided to lay my clothes out for the next day and then just get in the bed. I must have fell asleep because I was awakened by Kai'Juan pulling me to him. I didn't even try to stop him. I had to admit to myself, it felt good to be in his arms again.

"Kai?" I said softly.

"Yeah?"

"Why do you say you love me and then turn around and hurt me?" I asked and then turned to face him. He was silent for a minute and then looked at me. Even in the dark, I could feel the tension mixed with passion in the room.

"I really can't even answer that. I can't lie, I love the fuck out of you and I been hurt as fuck without you around, but at the same time, I love hoes. They just come so easily. They're not a challenge to me. You on the other hand, I have to work hard for, even though you always forgive me. I guess I just want both," he said honestly.

"But you can't have both. I'm tired of getting my heart broken," I said as the tears started to form. He sat up and turned on the light.

"Man don't cry. For real. You know I hate seeing you cry," Kai'Juan said wiping a tear from my cheek.

"I can't help it. The shit hurts. I'm starting to feel like this was a bad idea. I can't be around you without feeling some type of way. I should have never asked you to come with me," I said.

"Man stop all that. You know just like I know that we needed to have this conversation. I know you been wanting answers and I'm trying to be honest with you. I'm not gonna say that I want us to be back together, even though I do. I just want you to hear my side, no matter how dumb I sound," Kai'Juan said grabbing my hands. "I love you. PERIOD. I know I do dumb ass shit and I fuck up constantly but don't ever question how I feel about you. I'm sorry for constantly hurting you and I'm sorry for making you feel like you don't matter. You are the most important thing in my life. One day I'mma marry you and I'mma knock you up about a good 5 times," Kai'Juan said laughing.

"You got me fucked up," I said laughing with him.

"Nah but seriously Nae, I want us to be together. Just give me some time to make it right," he said staring in my eyes. I felt like he was burning a hole through my soul or some shit.

"Ok Kai'Juan. I'll give you a chance to make it right, but we aren't back together. You gotta show me something," I said.

"I know. I will. Just watch," he said.

"I'm watching," I replied. For the rest of the night, we laid in the dark...talking.

CHRIS

"*W*here you at?" I said into the phone. I had been sitting at this damn restaurant for 30 minutes waiting on Tasha's slow ass.

"Nigga don't rush me. I'm walking in now," she said.

"No, you ain't," I replied.

"How the fuck you know?" Tasha said from behind me. I chuckled.

"Get fucked up," I said to her and then hugged her.

"Ain't nobody worried about you," Tasha said laughing. She sat down as soon as the waitress came over to take our order. Lately, Tasha had been my stress reliever. Tammy had still been acting funny, but I was starting not to give a fuck. I know she was still fucking with Brandon and frankly, they could have each other. She wanted to play it crazy so that was fine. Of course, I love her and all but I'm not about to look stupid for nobody. I don't care how much I love you. Then she claimed she was pregnant but still fucking with his bitch ass. How could I think that baby was mine? I wanted to, but I didn't wanna be some lame ass nigga that let his girl walk all over him. Fuck that.

"So what you been up to ugly?" Tasha asked. We hadn't seen each other in about a week. The dealership kept me busy. It's crazy how

18

BRANDON

*T*ammy had really pissed me the fuck off that night at the beach, but I couldn't do shit but accept it. Shit, if she wanted to act like that, it was ok. But I'm sure Chris' soft ass wasn't enough for her and she'd be back. Nothing can compare to your first love. On my way to my house, my phone started vibrating. I glanced down at it in the cup holder and then answered it by pressing the button on my steering wheel.

"Yeah," I answered.

"Can you come get me?" the voice said sniffling.

"What the fuck wrong with you?" I asked the caller.

"Just come get me Brandon. I'll tell you later."

"Alright man, where you at?"

"At Outback."

"Nigga, which one?"

"The only one in the city dumb ass. Just come get me," she said and then hung up. About 10 minutes later I was pulling up and saw Tasha standing outside with a swollen cheek. She got in the car and I looked at her.

"Who the fuck beat yo ass?" I asked laughing. She punched me in the arm.

"That shit ain't funny," Tasha said.

"So, what happened? And where the fuck is your car?" I asked. Tasha went on to explain to me what went down between her, Chris and Anaya. I had to admit, Anaya was a beast. She didn't play when it came to Tammy, but I didn't know Chris had it in him to be sneaking around on Tammy like that.

"Damn, straight up? You seeing my enemy? That's some grimy ass shit," I said to her. I was kind of pissed off, but I really couldn't be.

"I know all about your plan. I'm trying to help you out since Lauren ass ain't. She's too emotional. Where you find that hoe?" she asked, and I laughed again. Tasha had always had a smart-ass mouth.

"Don't worry about it," I said.

"Brandon, I'm your wife. Your business is my business" she told me. I looked at her and laughed. This bitch had me fucked up.

"You said that with so much confidence. We are SEPERATED!" I stated, sounding out separated like she was retarded. "We've been that way for years. Stop acting like you don't know wassup," I said still laughing.

"I know that. But on paper, I'm still your wife, so I'm not tryna hear none of that bullshit. Together or not, you belong to me," she said.

"You really got me fucked up," I said.

"Do I?" she said smirking.

"Don't try to go down memory lane. I'm only barely fucking with you off the strength of Asia," I said. Asia was our 3-year-old and she was bad as hell, but she was my Princess. She could get anything that she wanted from me and I'm pretty sure that her little ass knew it. Technically, Imani was Asia's mother, but she never wanted to be a mom. She claimed she didn't have the "motherly instinct" and didn't want to screw up our kid.

I would always have love for Tasha for the simple fact that she took in my seed when she didn't have to, but at the same time, I couldn't stand her. When we were together, she kept harping on the fact that we were "shacking up" and basically forced me to marry her. At the time, I figured it was the right thing to do. Especially since we were raising Asia together. If I could take it back, I would've never let her talk me into it. Now I was stuck with her ass because she didn't want to sign the divorce papers.

Tasha thought she owned me but that couldn't be farther from the truth. She was a straight up savage to everybody but me and I couldn't roc with bitches who got down like she did. If anything, I owned her. She let me take control of her heart and her mind, and now that I had that, I could make her do whatever I wanted. Everything except get a divorce.

"Really? So that's the only reason why you still fuck with me?"

"Yup. And I barely wanna do that. You a grimy bitch and I regret the day I laid eyes on yo ass."

"Says the motherfucker who fucked his girlfriend's best friend and got her pregnant you fucking dummy!" she yelled. I pulled over automatically. She loved bringing that shit up like she was a saint or some shit. She had no idea that I knew ALL her secrets, but she would in time.

"You got one more time to talk to me crazy in my own car or I promise you I'll pull over and drop yo ass off on the side of the road. Better yet, how about I call up Anaya or Tammy to come finish fucking you up?" I said laughing. She really thought she had the upper hand, but she didn't.

"Ok Brandon," she said giving up.

"Good, now that we got that out the way, let's talk business. Since you the only motherfucker sticking to the plan, I gotta give you an update," I said glancing over at her. Her eyes damn near lit up.

"Talk to me," she said, and I started to run down my plan. Niggas didn't even see it coming but boy oh boy they were in for a surprise.

19

TAMMY

*A*fter getting off the phone with Anaya, I was pissed off, but I wasn't reacting how I thought I would. Surprisingly, I was calm as fuck. Maybe because I almost didn't give a fuck that Chris was out with another bitch. I mean, of course I cared because regardless he was still my man and I loved him, but a part of me already knew. Women always know when something isn't right. Usually Chris is soft when it came to me. He would do any and everything for me and I always had him wrapped around my little finger. Lately, he'd been acting funny; sneaking to talk on the phone, out all night, and he even put a passcode on his phone. Where they do that at? I never said anything about it because, let's face it, I was doing my dirt too. I heard the front door open and close and then I heard Chris call my name. I walked out of the bedroom and went to the front of the steps with my arms folded under my chest.

"Look, I know you probably pissed off, but hear me out first," Chris said.

"No, that's ok. You don't have to explain anything to me. Just don't be so sloppy with the hoe next time. I really don't feel like beating her ass, but you know I will," I told him walking away, but he followed me.

"Hold up, so that's all you have to say? You ok knowing another female has your man's attention?" he said firing question after question at me.

"To answer that last question, I'm already over it. I had my suspicions that you were out doing me dirty, but I never wanted to believe it because it's you. I know you love me Chris, but if you're not happy anymore I'm not going to beg you to stay with me," I said honestly. He frowned and looked at me with anger and hurt, like I'd just broke his heart. I felt bad looking in his eyes, but I didn't feel bad for speaking the truth.

"If I was really a hoe ass nigga I would choke the fuck out of you right now. I know the real. You so nonchalant because yo ass been on Brandon's dick ever since he popped back up. You know what; you two motherfuckers can have each other. I'm sick of walking around here acting like I don't know what it is between us. You got me out here looking stupid as fuck T. You been texting this nigga, going out with this nigga and you expect me to sit at home wondering where the fuck you at and who the you with like a bitch? You looking for anything you can get on me just to say that we don't have to be together. Then you drop a bomb one and tell me you're pregnant and you wonder why I'm questioning it? But that's cool. We don't have to be together and we won't. I'm done with you. I'll be back to get my stuff later this week. Don't be here when I come and don't come crawling to me when his bitch ass breaks your heart again," he said and then walked out the door slamming it. I just stood there with my mouth open for a minute, in complete shock. What the fuck just happened?

20

TASHA

*L*oud banging on my door woke me up from the sleep I was in.

"Damn it!" I said throwing the covers off of myself. Who the fuck is banging on my damn door like that? I thought to myself. If this is Brandon, I just might have to cut him. I swung the door open without looking through the peep hole to see who it was. I was pleasantly surprised to see Chris.

"What are you doing here?" I asked.

"I left Tammy. Can I come in?" he asked looking like a sad puppy. He literally looked like he witnessed his dog get run over by a car.

"Of course, you can. Come on in," I said stepping to the side to let him in. "Why'd you leave her?" I asked getting straight to the point. I wanted to hear everything. Him leaving Tammy was like music to my ears.

He sat on the couch and then I joined him. He stared off into space for a minute and then proceeded to tell me everything. When he told me that she and Brandon were back fucking around I wanted to go whoop both of their asses. That hoe had some type of spell over his ass, especially when they were together. I can recall several times in the beginning of our relationship where he slipped up and called me Tammy. He even told me that he was secretly waiting on her ass to come back to him and if she ever did he was leaving me. Why even go as far as marrying me if you wanted another bitch? If he knew that he really didn't want to be with me, why the fuck was he playing house with me? I was literally fuming on the inside. Just wait until I see Brandon, or better yet, wait until I see Tammy.

"Tasha, you listening?" Chris said interrupting my trip down memory lane.

"I'm sorry, I honestly wasn't paying attention. What were you saying?" I asked sounding concerned. I really didn't give a fuck about his relationship with the bitch, and quite frankly Chris' whiny ass was starting to get on my fucking nerves. At first, I was starting to like him, but this side of him was turning me completely off. I think that he thinks we're gonna be together but that's the last thing on my mind. He can't even handle Tammy; I know damn well he can't handle me. I hoped Brandon held up his end of the bargain because I don't know how long I can play my role.

21

KAI'JUAN

a nigga was happy as shit. I had finally got my girl back, well not really but damn near. The trip to the family reunion was fun as hell. Her family was crazy as fuck and funny. They were really like my second family. I could tell Janae was happy too, her ass hadn't stop smiling since the first night when I poured my heart out like a bitch. I guess it was ok to be sensitive to your girl when you love her. I was determined to make shit right with her ass. No more fucking these rat bitches. It was all about Janae and my money. I really didn't have any family except my brother and I made sure that lil nigga was straight at all times. I didn't play about mines. I looked over at Janae and I felt like I was looking at her for the first time. A nigga was really in love with her pretty ass.

"Stop staring at me you creep," Janae said in a sleepy voice. I chuckled.

"How you know I'm looking at you?" I asked.

"I can feel it" she said turning over so that she was facing me.

"Yo, that's some weird ass shit," I said laughing.

"What's so funny?"

"I was just thinking that a nigga done got soft as fuck quick as hell."

"And it only took you 3 years of fucking over me," she said sarcastically.

"I thought we were trying to get past all that?" I asked.

"We are. I'm just reminding you," she said sticking her tongue out at me then getting out of the bed and heading to the bathroom.

"You better put your tongue back in your mouth unless you plan on sucking something," I said playfully. She laughed.

"Get out my face boy," she said closing the door.

"Aye, that's rude as fuck to close the door in somebody's face like that. Hurry up in there. I don't have all day waiting on your girly ass to get dressed," I said raising my voice a little, so she could hear me through the closed bathroom door and the music playing on her phone.

"Shut up. I'll be ready when I'm ready," she said. I laughed to myself. She wasn't ever ready in a decent amount of time. EVER. I was packing up our stuff when I felt my phone vibrate in my pocket. I looked at it and groaned, it was a text message from Lauren.

Lauren: Hey Baby

Me: What you want Lauren?

Lauren: I haven't heard from you all weekend. Everything straight?

Me: Yeah everything good. I been with my girl at her family reunion

Lauren: What girl?

Me: Janae. Who else?

Lauren: That bitch is not your girl no more.

Me: Chill out with that bitch word

Lauren: So y'all back together?

Me: Yup. Now stop texting my phone, matter of fact, delete my shit from your phone. I'm good on you

Lauren: Fuck you

Me: You wish you still could

I shook my head and then put my phone down on the night stand beside the bed. This crazy bitch was gonna be a problem. I just might have Janae beat her ass one good time and get her off me. Or I might just kill the bitch. About 20 minutes later, Janae came out the bathroom in just a towel and started getting dressed. She walked over to the night stand to grab her lotion and then my phone started ringing. She scrunched her face up, so I already knew who it was.

"Kai your hoes are calling," she said walking away with an attitude.

"Answer it," I told her.

"What?" she asked looking shocked. I never let anybody answer my shit and she knew it. But I figured that I don't have shit to hide anymore so why not? She could call every bitch in my contacts for all I cared. That just made my job easier. But seemed like bitches wanted you more when they knew you had a girl. Shit was ass backwards, but that's how these hoes thought.

"Answer it. I don't have shit to hide from you no more. Let that bitch know we back together and I'm through fucking with her. I told her silly ass once already, but you know bitches is kind of slow," I said. "I'm about to go put these bags in the car really quick. I'll be right back," I said then walked out the room.

22

JANAE

I think Kai'Juan was on drugs or some shit. I don't know what got in to him, but he's been acting brand new. I was really shocked at his behavior, but in a good way. He's becoming a totally different man right before my eyes, I just hoped that this change was permanent.

Even though he told me to answer his phone, I didn't want to. I was gonna let him handle his own business with his bitches and leave it at that. At least, I tried to do that, but the bitch KEPT calling, non-stop and it was annoying. I picked up the phone and answered it.

"Hello?"

"Let me speak to Kai'Juan," Lauren said with an attitude.

"Bitch I'mma tell you one time and one time only. Kai'Juan is mine and is always gonna be mine. Know your place hoe. I was asked to relay a message. He says he's good on you. Call my man's phone again and it's gonna be a problem. That's not a threat either, it's a promise," I said and then hung up.

"You a fake ass thug, you know that?" Kai'Juan said teasing me. "That's not a threat either, it's a promise," he said mocking me. I laughed and tossed him his phone.

"Fuck you. Let's go, I'm hungry," I said grabbing my purse and overnight bag before heading out the door.

"You one hungry motherfucker. You pregnant?" he asked. I stopped dead in my tracks.

"If I am I must be having Jesus' baby. You know I'm on birth control," I said.

"Oh yeah, you right," Kai'Juan said remembering. We hopped in the car and were on our way back to the city. I was ready to get home.

23

TAMMY

*I*t had been four days since Chris walked out on me. I wanted to be sad, but I wasn't, and I felt bad about it. I felt like I should be curled up in a corner crying but I felt just fine. Well, besides the fact that this baby was kicking my ass. I was only 8 weeks pregnant, but I felt like I was 8 months. This throwing up shit was not cool.

"Yo that's like the third time you done threw up since I been here T. You good?" Brandon asked me. He came over to keep me some company since I had called off of work. I just wasn't feeling it.

"B, I gotta tell you something," I said.

"Wassup?"

"Ummm...I'm pregnant," I finally told him.

"By Chris?" he asked. I slapped him upside the head.

"Who the fuck else Brandon?" I yelled.

"Damn, you bitchy already? I was just asking," he said laughing a little.

"It's not fucking funny. I don't even know if I wanna keep this baby. Chris is gone, and I'm not fit to be a single mother B," I said sitting on the bed.

"First of all, don't let no stupid shit like that come out your mouth again. You keeping this baby. If you pregnant it's for a reason. I wish you would. And you won't be alone. I know fasho Chris gone take care of his seed. He may be a bitch ass nigga but I gotta give credit where it's due, he'd be a good father and you know it. Plus, you got me," he said.

"I don't know. I wanna talk to Chris about it but he won't answer my calls or texts. Laid up with some bitch named Tasha," I ranted. Then I thought about it...Tasha was the name of my new patient. Nah, it's no way. It's a million Tasha's in the world. My patient Tasha had an appointment with me tomorrow and I really want to ask her, but that would be so unprofessional.

"You know what she look like?" Brandon asked.

"No. Why does that even matter?" I questioned.

"It doesn't. I was just wondering. I might know her," he said. I gave him a look.

"Don't play with me. If you know the hoe I'm fucking, you up," I said seriously.

"Why you fucking me up? I don't even know if I know her," he said.

"Because if you do then that means that you knew and that makes me look like a dumb ass."

"Shut up T. Don't nobody know that girl. You thinking way too much little dog," Brandon said getting off the bed. "Come on prego. Let's go grab something to eat," he said grabbing my hand and walking me to the door.

"I am hungry as hell," I said.

"That ain't nothing new."

* * *

THE NEXT DAY, I was sitting at my desk anticipating Tasha's appointment that was in five minutes. I really hoped that the Tasha that Chris is messing around with isn't the same Tasha that's about to step foot in this office. The things that girl was telling me about her past, I would hate for Chris to get wrapped up in it. We may not be together anymore, but I didn't want anything to happen to him. I still cared about him. That just doesn't go away. Knock Knock!

"Come in!" I said.

"Ms. Stevenson, your 2:30 is here," my secretary said.

"Thank you, send her in," I said. I was nervous, and I really didn't understand why. She was just one of my patients. No big deal. Tasha came in, and gave me a weak smile before sitting down on the couch while I took a seat across from her in my huge lounge chair. I liked to be comfortable at work.

"Hi Tasha, how are you this afternoon?" I asked her.

"I could be a lot better doc," Tasha said sadly.

"Well, what's wrong? Give me an update. At our last meeting you were telling me about you and your husband. Have things gotten any better?" I asked her.

"No, they've actually gotten worse. He just won't let me leave but he doesn't want me. Every time I bring up a divorce he cuts me off. He has me doing some things I really don't want to do," Tasha said almost on the verge of tears.

"Things like what?" I asked trying to get more information out of her.

"Well, he has this plan that I can't really talk about and he has me involved in it and I honestly just want out," she said with the tears now streaming down her face.

"Have you told him this?" I asked.

"Yes of course I have but he threatens to take my baby from me any time I go against what he says," she said sobbing.

"Don't cry. The only advice I have for you is to pray on it and ask God to give you the strength. Don't allow a man to have that much power over you. Your husband sounds super controlling. I know you may not want to get the police involved, but if he's really this bad, you need to protect yourself. As long as you have a vagina, you hold the power. Remember that," I said to her.

"Thanks Doc," she said. "I really appreciate you."

"No problem. By the way Tasha, I have a question for you," I said. I was honestly nervous as hell. I was afraid of the answer that I might get but I was also afraid to lose my license. I just needed to know what was going on.

"Sure, go ahead," she said crossing her legs from one side to the other.

"Do you know someone named Chris? He kind of looks like Michael Ealy, just with light brown eyes?" I asked. Tasha shifted in her seat a little bit. That right there told me the answer.

"Yeah, I know Chris, he sold me my car," she said. "Why do you ask?" The way that she was shifting in her seat and making sure that she didn't lock eyes was me was suspicious as fuck and I wanted to whoop her ass.

"Just curious," I said keeping it short. I was kind of pissed because I now knew who Chris was spending all his time with. I couldn't even hate. The chick was gorgeous.

After Tasha left, I decided to leave work early. That's what I liked about being a therapist. There was never a set time for me to come in to work. Only when I had appointments scheduled. As I was walking out of the building, I heard my name being called. I turned to my left and saw Chris leaning against his car. I walked over to him.

"Wassup baby mama?" Chris said greeting me. I rolled my eyes.

"Please don't call me that," I said in an irritated way.

"Why? You are my baby's mama. I mean, that is my baby, right?" Chris said smirking. Lately, he'd been a real asshole towards me and I was tempted to slap the shit out of him.

"I really wanna slap the shit out of you right now. Today is not the day to be fucking with me Christopher."

"Man chill out with that Christopher shit," he said to me.

"I'm starting to think you and Kai'Juan done switched places. All of a sudden you're an ass and he all in love and soft," I said.

"You calling me soft?" he asked.

"Towards me you were," I said honestly.

"And you see where that shit got me," he said with an attitude.

"Ok Chris, did you come here to get on my nerves and argue? What's the reason for this unpleasant surprise?" I asked.

"I know I been ignoring you lately and I apologize. It was childish.

wish she would go back to where she came from. I liked pretending she didn't exist.

"Why?" I questioned her. I needed to know what her purpose was. If he thought about adding her to this plan, I was going to have a real problem. She looked at me and laughed like I had said something funny. She got up from the couch and walked over to me. Imani was about 5'7" and was thick as hell. Brandon always did have a thing about big booties, so I understood why he was attracted to her. She reminded me of the singer Ciara in the face. I had to admit, the bitch was bad, but she had so much attitude and so much mouth, it made me hate her. Not to mention the foul shit she did when she fucked Brandon behind Tammy's back. Granted, I couldn't stand Tammy's ass either but even I wasn't that damn grimy towards any of my friends. There were some lines you just didn't cross.

"He wants me to try and rebuild my friendship with Tammy. I can't lie, I miss my bitch. But I know T, she gone try to beat my ass," she laughed a little. I don't know why she thought getting her ass whooped was funny.

"Why did he bring you here? He couldn't put your ass in a hotel or something? I don't fuck with you and both of y'all know that," I said folding my arms. I really didn't like this hoe.

"Hell if I know. Ask him," she said shrugging and then walking away. I rolled my eyes. This wasn't going to work out. I was gonna end up beating her ass.

25

BRANDON

I feel like I'm the realist nigga alive. What nigga you know got his wife and his baby mama under the same roof, knowing they don't fuck with each other. I really didn't feel like spending no cash on no hotel room for Imani, but I was thinking about it though. I knew eventually Tasha's ass was gonna call me cussing me the fuck out for letting Imani in her crib. I'll give it a few days and see how it goes with the two of them. I might make it even sooner with the way she was looking when I came to pick her up from the airport. Those gray leggings and that white wife beater did something to me. It was so simple but damn! I shouldn't even be thinking about her ass like that, but Tammy was playing, and Imani would gladly throw the pussy at me. I pulled my phone out to text Tammy. I wanted to take her out tonight, and I was hoping she wouldn't hoe me.

Me: Yo T

Tammy: Yeah?

Me: What you doing?

Tammy: Shit. Chillin, watching Netflix. What you up to?

Me: Nothing much. I was thinking about you, I wanted to take you out to dinner or something.

Tammy: Sure B, I'm always down to eat lol

Me: You greedy. Be ready in about an hour. I'll text you when I'm outside

Tammy: OK

Finally! Shit! That girl had been acting a little funny, but I guess she was back to the old T. Plus I knew her greedy ass was hungry because not only could she eat but that baby could put away some food. I was kind of excited too.

I pulled up in front of Tasha's apartment complex and got out. I was gonna have to make it a point to come visit a couple times a week now that Imani was there. As I got closer to Tasha's floor I started to hear what sounded like two people arguing and when I stepped off the elevator, the voices became clear; Tasha and Imani. I shook my head and jogged down the hallway until I got to Tasha's door and then started banging on it like I was the police. These hoes hadn't even been in the same space for 24 hours yet and already it was a problem. After a few bangs on the door, Tasha swung the door open.

"Get this bitch out my shit NOW Brandon! What the fuck is wrong with your stupid ass?" Tasha screamed at me.

"Aye man chill the fuck out. What the fuck happened?" I said, entering the apartment. Tasha's ass got on my last damn nerves, but she had good taste. The living room along with her bedroom and bathroom were decorated with black furniture and accented with royal blue pillows, area rugs and other accessories. Shit was cold as hell, I had to admit.

"This bitch all in my bed like it's her shit. I told her to get the fuck up and go in the guest bedroom and she caught an attitude, like she ain't in my house. Petty ass," Tasha fussed. I gave her a look that let her know I was irritated. Women were so petty, they would argue over anything that they could argue over.

"Man. Come on Imani let's go. I'm not about to deal with this bull-shit!" I said agitated.

"Where we going?" she asked.

"Just get your shit and come the fuck on," I said in a serious tone.

A few moments later she was walking towards the door with 3 large duffle bags and her oversized Louis Vuitton bag.

"Thank you. You shoulda never brought her ass here in the first place," Tasha said under her breath.

"Yo Tash, chill out before I beat yo ass. That smart ass mouth ain't gone get you nowhere," I said and slammed the door on my way out. I heard Tasha yelling still, but I paid her ass no mind. She'd be alright eventually.

On the way to the hotel, Imani just wouldn't shut the fuck up.

"B, I miss you. I know I haven't been around but I'm ready to come back to where I belong," she rambled.

"Man shut the fuck up! This is exactly why I'm never coming back. You talk too fucking much and you petty as hell. I don't have time for your bullshit Imani. You here to help me out and then I'm shipping your ass back where you came from," I said to her.

"You really got me fucked up. I don't have to do shit. You ain't my fucking Daddy motherfucker!" she said. I just closed my mouth. I didn't feel like arguing with this broad. I had to focus. Whether I wanted to admit it or not, without Imani and Tasha, I didn't have a plan at all. I had to play it smart, so I decided to be nice to the girls for now. If they weren't my baby's mamas I would off they asses as soon as all this was over.

26

KAI'JUAN

*W*ithout Chris being my right-hand man, I was doing everything my fucking self in these streets and it was starting to stress me the fuck out. B wasn't really helping, he was just supplying me with the product. I would think since he was my dog, he would be tryna help, but then again, I forgot who the fuck I was talking about. Brandon was one selfish ass nigga. Even though he was my friend and we were close, I couldn't trust him the way I could trust Chris.

"What you over there thinking about boss?" one of my corner boys, Damani said to me. He'd been working for me for a little over two years. He was a lil nigga, 19 years old, but he was loyal. He already had at least 3 bodies under his belt. The little nigga was not to be fucked with.

"My bad lil nigga. I was thinking about some shit, obviously," I said and laughed a little bit.

"Well snap out of it. We gotta handle this shit right quick," he said to me. Word on the street was that niggas over on the east side had been hitting our stash houses little by little. It had to be an inside job and I wasn't for that unloyal shit. I called my entire team and had them meet me at the warehouse, so we could straighten shit out. One thing my crew knew, if we were meeting at the warehouse, somebody wasn't leaving. I looked at Damani and nodded my head and he began walking down the hallway that led to the meeting room inside the warehouse.

Once we walked through the doors, all conversation ceased. That type of shit always made me feel like a true boss. I loved when all eyes were on me. I looked around at all my soldiers, trying to figure out who the snake was, but I couldn't pinpoint it. Every single man that I had around me had gone through a thorough background check. Not only that, but these were niggas that had been around me since day one. Well, most of them. Damani and this other cat Rico were the rookies out of everybody. I looked back at Damani and he gave me a slight nod that let me know he had my back. I took my spot at the large round table and began to speak.

"As you all know, I don't hold meetings in this warehouse for nothing. One of you niggas has proven to be disloyal and I want to know who is stupid enough to go against me," I said in a calm but demanding tone. I paused to give someone a chance to speak up, but no one did.

"Oh, so y'all gone bitch up on me?" I said pulling my gun from my waist. A couple nigga's eyes got big, but they tried to play it off. I aimed my gun at Rico.

"Rico, you were the one watching the spot-on Mendota so please explain to me how the fuck you lost track of 20 bands and 10 keys?" I asked giving him a look that let him know he only had one chance to answer.

"K, on God I..." he started but I shot him right in between his eyes. I wasn't the one to be fucked with. That nigga was about to lie through his teeth and I just couldn't take it.

"The next time you niggas think it's okay to steal from me, let this motherfucker be an example to you," I said pointing my gun at Rico's body. "I'll kill all you niggas and go buy some more. Tighten the fuck up before all y'all Mamas and Baby Mamas be in the church crying over y'all. Do I make myself clear?" I yelled. They all nodded their head in agreement and I walked out of the room with Damani. I didn't have time for niggas to be fucking up my money, but I wasn't worried, I was going to handle it one way or another.

27

TAMMY

*C*hris said that he would be there through this pregnancy and help me with this baby, but here I was at my first doctor's appointment by my damn self. I know that he knew all about the appointment because I'd texted him the time and location two days ago and he responded saying that he'd be here, but he wasn't. A light knock on the door caused me to look up from my phone. The doctor stuck her head in before entering the room, smiling.

"How are you doing Ms. Samuels?" she asked going over to the sink and washing her hands.

"I'm good Doc, how are you?" I asked.

"I'm good, can't complain. I hear that congratulations are in order?" she said beaming. At 55 years old, Dr. Alexa Cunningham had been my OB/GYN since I was 18 years old, and I loved her. She was an attractive older woman, standing about 5'7", 160lbs, she was curvy but slim at the same time. What you call slim thick. She had salt and pepper hair, but it was always laid! This time, she had it in a natural wrap with tight curls which complemented her milk chocolate skin.

"Yes, I'm so nervous Dr. Worthy. I've never been pregnant, so I don't know how this is supposed to go. The only thing that I know is what I read on the internet from other pregnant women. I've been throwing up, I always feel nauseous. I just want to lay in the bed and eat all day," I said laughing lightly, and she laughed as well.

"That's normal, especially for women in their first trimester. If you like, I can prescribe you some nausea pills. In the meantime, let's take a look at the little peanut, shall we?" she said grabbing this computer on wheels that I know was used for ultrasounds. After scooting her chair over to me, she told me to put my legs in the stirrups. Once my legs were up, she entered a few things on the computer and grabbed this device that looked like a dick, and put a condom on it. I don't know if it was actually a condom, but it definitely looked like it.

"What is that?" I asked her.

"It's called a transducer. We use it for women who aren't too far along. A lot of times, we aren't able to see the baby using the normal transducer because of the size of the fetus, so we use this in the beginning stages. We would use the same thing if we were looking for something more serious in your uterus," she explained. She squirted some gel on the transducer and let me know that I may feel a little pressure before inserting it in my vagina. Just like I thought, it felt like a dick. I know I was probably a pervert for even thinking sexually during my first sonogram, but that's how it felt. Dr. Worthy swirled the transducer around for a few minutes while looking at the screen. I started to panic, thinking that something could be wrong with my baby.

"Is everything ok Doc?" I asked with concern. I lifted up a bit to try and see what was going on, even though I had no clue what I was looking at.

"Yes, everything is fine sweetheart. Your baby is already active. Every time I find him or her it moves. I'm trying to catch the baby off guard so that I can find the heartbeat and see how far along you are," she said with a reassuring smile. I breathed a sigh of relief and laid back.

"Thank God. I was scared for a minute there," I said.

"Don't be, because listen," she said and then I heard the sound of my baby's heart beat for the first time ever. It was fast paced and steady and it was the greatest sound I'd ever heard. Tears welled up in my eyes as I thought about bringing a child into this world. A whole human being that was created out of love, between me and Chris.

"Oh my God!" I stated as the tears started to fall.

"The heartbeat is very strong, which is good. It seems that you're about 10 weeks along, so your due date will be on or around February 19th. It's too soon to know if the baby is a boy or girl. We'll find that out at your 16-week checkup. Hopefully the baby will be acting right, and we can find out the gender on the first try. Do you and Chris want to know the gender immediately or are you doing a gender reveal? By the way, where is Chris?" she asked, and I rolled my eyes.

"We're going through a few things right now. I thought he would be here, but I guess he couldn't make it," I said shrugging my shoulders. Dr. Worthy nodded her head before taking the transducer out of me and cleaning me off.

"Well, I hope you guys work things out. You and baby are looking good from my end. I'll print out a few pictures for you to take home and then we will go ahead and set up your next appointment. I'll also prescribe you your prescription for your prenatal vitamins as well as the nausea pills," she said. I sat up on the table and nodded my head in agreement.

"I definitely need those pills Doc," I said.

"I got you covered. Go ahead and get dressed and the receptionist will give you your prescriptions and schedule your next appointment. Try not to stress too much!" she said walking out of the door.

I hopped off the table and started to get dressed. Once I had my clothes on, I fished around in my purse for my keys, but noticed that my cell phone was vibrating, indicating that I had a text message. I looked at my iPhone screen and saw Chris's name pop up. I instantly rolled my eyes and put my phone back in my purse. Now this nigga wants to text me? How ironic. I got my keys out of my purse then walked out of the room to the front desk to get my prescriptions and schedule my next appointment.

I'm still in shock that I was about to be someone's mother. I knew that sooner or later one of us was going to have to move out of the

"That's Wassup T. I'm happy for you baby girl," he said, and I smiled. This is the kind of support I need around me.

"Thanks B. So, Wassup? I know you didn't call just to chit chat," I said getting to the reason for him calling.

"I didn't want shit. I was really just calling to check up on you, that's all. Oh, and I wanted to see if you wanted to hang out Friday night. I know you can't drink and stuff, but I also know if nobody drags you, yo ass will be in the house for the rest of your life. It's okay to get out and have some fun. So whatever you want to do, just let me know, alright?" he stated.

"Yeah, that's cool B. I appreciate that."

"No problem baby girl. I'll hit you up later," he said and then disconnected the call abruptly. As soon as I was starting to doubt if me & Brandon's relationship could be strictly platonic, he just confirmed that it can. It felt good to have a male in my corner. I used to think that the only male in my life I'd ever need is Chris and my Daddy, but damn how quickly things change.

28

IMANI

I'm so tired of being stuck in this funky ass hotel room. Brandon brought me all the way here just to stash me somewhere and forget all about me. I'm nobody's puppet, and I wasn't about to sit here like some obedient pet waiting on its master to return home, fuck that. In fact, I missed my baby and I wanted to spend some time with her. Tasha's ass ran off and got Brandon to marry her and then had the nerve to raise MY baby as hers. That's what I call bullshit. I couldn't stand Tasha for the simple fact that she took my life. Yes, at the time I was not ready to be somebody's mother, so I left her with her Daddy and went to live my life. Now, I'm starting to see that was a big mistake. Brandon wouldn't even let me go near my baby. He said he didn't want to "confuse her," which instantly made me feel like Asia didn't know who I was at all. Asia only had one mother and that was me.

I paced the floor for the thousandth time thinking about how to get the hell out of here. I had no money, no phone and no car. I was fucked. I went over to the window and just looked out, admiring the view of Detroit. This city was fucked up a lot of times, but it was still home to me. I'd always thought that downtown looked beautiful at night. I stared out of the window for a few more seconds until a thought hit me. I quickly grabbed the room key and went out the door. I knew what I was going to do.

29

CHRIS

I had been staying with Tasha for a few days, especially after missing Tammy's first doctor's appointment today. At first, Tasha's place was a nice little get away from all this bullshit going on between Tammy and I, but now, I just wanted to go the fuck home. Tasha was cool and everything, but she was starting to act like my presence was annoying her, and I didn't stay anywhere that I wasn't wanted. I was low key being a bitch because I didn't want to deal with whatever was coming to me once I got home, but I had to at least talk to Tammy and figure out where we stood.

"Tash, I'm about to head out," I said getting up from the couch and heading towards the door. She didn't respond, but I left anyway. I jumped in my truck and headed in the direction of me and Tammy's house, which was about 10 minutes away. I didn't know if she was home, and I hadn't bothered to call or text her, I just wanted to catch her off guard. That way she wouldn't have time to plan out what she was going to say to me. I just wanted this conversation to be raw, no matter what the outcome may be.

After a few more minutes, I pulled into the driveway and killed the engine. Tammy's car wasn't in the driveway, but that didn't surprise me, because she always parked her car in the garage. I hopped out of my truck and made my way towards the front door. I used my key to unlock the door and was grateful that she hadn't changed the locks. Once I entered the house, I heard the sound of the TV coming from the living room. I walked past the office, dining room and kitchen and found Tammy sitting on the couch engrossed in Love & Hip Hop. I really don't understand how females love this garbage.

"Tam," I said, making my presence known. She jumped up quick, knocking a bowl of apple slices over. She looked at me and then placed her hand over her chest, breathing heavily.

"You scared the shit out of me Chris! What are you doing here?" she asked, bending over to pick up the bowl of fruit that she'd dropped. I watched her for a few seconds, just admiring her, before I responded to her question. Even in the high waist yoga leggings, an oversized shirt and her hair in a messy bun, Tammy was still beautiful. I hoped that our baby was a girl and looked just like her Mommy. I wanted her to act like her Mommy too. Tammy wasn't perfect, but she was the closest thing to it. I know that I tripped out on her for talking to Brandon, even though I was talking to Tasha on the low, but I'm starting to realize that the grass is definitely not greener on the other side. I couldn't lie and say that I didn't love and miss this woman because I definitely did. I just hoped that she still wanted to make it work, because I did.

"I just came over to talk to you. I know that you're probably pissed at me for missing the appointment today and I wanted to apologize. I also wanted us to sit down and have this much-needed conversation. We need to figure out what we're going to do as far as our relationship and this baby," I stated, and she nodded her head.

"I agree, we do need to have a conversation. Come sit down, we can talk," she said sitting back down and patting the couch. I walked over to the couch and sat down facing her. She folded her legs Indian style and faced me, then just looked at me, waiting for me to speak up first. I took a deep breath and prepared myself for this.

"Ok, T, look, I know that we've been going through a lot lately and I know that I haven't been a good boyfriend to you, but I want you to know that I'm still the same nigga. I definitely could have gone about things differently, but I want you to know that I still love you and I always will. You are my first love and the love of my life no matter what. I'm sorry that I doubted you and I'm sorry that I doubted this baby," I said touching her stomach, making a point.

"You mean the world to me and I want you to know that I want to be with you. I want to make this work, no matter what it takes. I still want to marry you and I still see the future that we've always talked about, but I know that you also have some of your own shit to deal with, and that's cool. Whatever you want to do, we can do. If you don't want to be with me, we can co-parent and be friends. If you want to be with me, we can make it work. It's whatever you want. I will meet you halfway on whatever you feel is best. Just let me know," I said sincerely. I looked at Tammy and she had tears coming down her cheeks. I didn't know if they were good tears or bad tears, and that kind of scared me. We sat there staring at each other for at least 3 minutes until she finally said something.

"Chris, I really don't even know what to say. I do love you, but I've honestly been okay without you and I feel bad about it. I feel bad that I'm not depressed and that I haven't been crying over us. I mean yes, I got mad when I found out that you've been kicking it with another bitch but at the same time I couldn't even blame you because I haven't been around. I honestly don't know what I want to do right now. I don't know if I want to be by myself or be with you. I need time to figure it out. As far as this baby, I would really appreciate it if we could still be friends at this time and if you could help me through this pregnancy. I mean, it's been easy so far besides the nausea, but I know that I can't do this by myself. I have Anaya, and my family and friends but it's nothing like the support of the person who helped you make the baby, you know?" she said, and I nodded my head.

I don't know why but I was expecting her to cry, say she loved me and that we would work it out and everything would be all good, but I didn't get that. I really didn't get much of anything from her. What the fuck does *I don't know* mean? It's so much that I could say to her right now, but I'll keep my comments to myself.

"I get it. I'll give you your space. I just wanted you to know where I stand," I said standing up to leave.

"Where are you going?" Tammy asked curiously.

"What you mean? I'm bouta go and give you your space," I said shrugging.

"Nigga I didn't mean space right now. I just wanted you to know that I don't have it all together right now. Come sit down and chill with me. What, we can't do that either?" she said sarcastically.

"Yeah, we can do that Tam," I said and sat back down. I grabbed the remote and pressed play. The Real Housewives showed up on the screen and I shook my head and changed the channel.

"Why you do that?" Tammy asked.

"We ain't watching this shit Tam, hell naw. We can watch a movie or something but I'm not watching this bullshit," I said, and she laughed.

"Ok, we can watch a movie," she said and went into the kitchen. A few minutes later she returned with a bowl of popcorn. For the rest of the night we sat in the living room, talking shit, eating junk and watching movies. It felt good to just chill with her and I hoped that I'd get my girl back, but for now, I was just happy to have my friend. Call me soft if you want, but it was nothing better than this.

30

KAI'JUAN

"Janae, I need you to come on man, damn!" I said yelling up the stairs for Janae. I told her hours ago to get ready and she still wasn't ready. I don't understand how it takes so fucking long to put on some pants, shoes, and a shirt. Women just had to take all day to do every fucking thing.

"Nigga don't rush me, I'm coming, damn! It takes time to be fine," she said, and I shook my head.

"You don't need all that make up and shit Nae. You look good no matter what. Now hurry the fuck up. I'm hungry as hell!" I said and laid down on the bed. I took my phone out and scrolled through my Instagram, waiting on Janae to *get fine*. Whatever the fuck that means.

I sat there scrolling through my Instagram for a few more minutes and finally Janae came out the bathroom. I glanced at her and then back at my phone, but I had to do a double take. My baby looked good as hell. She knows damn well that I loved when she wore black. She had on an all-black onesie pantsuit thing. I don't know what it was, but she looked good as hell. The top of her jumpsuit was off the shoulder and had some ruffle like shit. Her hair was parted down the middle with soft curls and her beautiful milk chocolate face was glowing. She looked so good I didn't even want to go out to eat no more. I licked my lips while she put on her heels.

I just watched her for a minute and I had to admit, I felt a little guilty. This whole time I've been fucking around on her with these nothing ass broads. I never stopped to think about what I was doing to her mentally and emotionally. I was just doing whatever the fuck I wanted to do because I knew I could get away with it.

"Why you staring at me like a weirdo?" Janae asked standing at the foot of the bed. I smirked and licked my lips.

"You just look good as fuck. I can't stare at my girl?"

"You can I guess. Thank you, baby," she chuckled. "Come on bae, I'm ready to go. I'm hungry as hell now," she said walking out of the room. I grabbed my phone and hopped out of the bed.

"Now you hungry but just ten minutes ago you was taking your sweet little time," I said looking down at my phone. I was about to turn it off for a while, but something caught my eye. I stopped walking and looked at the screen again to make sure my eyes weren't playing tricks on me. The more I stared at the picture the more confused I became.

"Kai!" Janae shouted from downstairs. I heard her talking but I couldn't even form the words to respond to her. "What the hell is wrong with you?" she asked. I didn't even notice that she had come upstairs. I looked up at her and then handed her the phone. She looked at me like I was crazy, took the phone from my hand and looked at the picture. Her confused expression turned into shock and she looked back up at me.

"How the fuck do these hoes know each other? And who is the other one?" she asked. Those were the exact questions that I kept asking myself, but I couldn't come up with the answer.

"I don't know, but we bouta find out," I said walking past her and going downstairs. I don't know why, but I had a real bad feeling about this shit.

"What you mean we're about to find out?" Janae asked following me.

"We about to pay these hoes a visit," I said, and Janae nodded in agreement. I was getting to the bottom of whatever the fuck was going on. These hoes were so fucking stupid, they added their location to the picture, so I was about to pay their dumb asses a visit. As I drove towards the restaurant, I couldn't help but to feel like this was a set up. I don't know how these bitches knew each other or where this third bitch came from, but I wanted some fucking answers. It didn't make any sense and I hated feeling like I was being left in the dark. I dialed up a few of my soldiers, including Damani, just in case I needed back up. You could never be too careful. Especially with the scandalous bitches we were about to encounter.

We pulled up to the Red Lobster after about fifteen minutes of driving and I jogged towards the entrance. At the same time that Kai'Juan and Janae were walking towards the entrance. I spotted them in a booth which was tucked away in the corner. Almost like they were hiding. They weren't even paying attention to their surroundings until we were just a few feet away. Lauren's ass was the first to look up since she was the one facing us. Her eyes got wide, which caused Imani and some other bitch to look up. I smirked as she made eye contact with me and then looked at Janae. I looked over at my baby and she looked like she wanted to kill her, which was understandable, but now was not the time nor the place. We had plenty of time for Janae to let out whatever frustrations she needed to. Right now, I just needed these hoes to leave this restaurant peacefully. I didn't want to cause a scene and I damn sure didn't want these white motherfuckers calling the police on my ass, which I knew they'd do in a heartbeat.

"If you bitches know what's good for you, you'll follow me outside," I stated in a calm but stern tone. They looked at me and then looked at each other for a moment before calmly sliding out of the booth. I stopped them as a thought came to me. "Before we start walking, give me your phones," I said, and they complied.

We all walked towards the entrance, and when we got there I noticed that there were 2 black escalades parked right at the door which caused me to smirk. My team always came through. As we walked out of the door, I instructed Lauren, Imani and the other girl to get in the trucks. I was still confused about who this third bitch was, but that was the least of my worries. All I wanted was answers. Mainly I just wanted to know how the fuck these two bitches knew each other. I guess I could've just sat down at the booth and talked to them like a regular human being, but fuck it. I liked my way better. Neither one of these bitches deserved to be treated like regular humans. The way I was feeling right now, I could kill both of them with my bare hands.

After I got the girls in the car, I made my way towards my car where Janae was. It dawned on me where I knew the third girl from. I knew she looked familiar, but I couldn't put my finger on it until now. She's been to the dealership a few times for whatever reason. I still didn't know her name, but I definitely knew her face. As I got into the car, I looked over at Janae and I could tell she was heated. She looked like she was just ready for whatever and that made me smile. My baby was a rider, but I know she had her own reasons for wanting to fuck some shit up too. I grabbed my phone and texted Chris to let him know what was going on and to meet me at our secret location. I waited a few minutes for him to text back, and once I got confirmation that he was on the way, I pulled out of the Red Lobster parking lot and started to drive. After about fifteen minutes of driving in silence, Janae finally spoke up.

"Where are we going?" she asked.

"The warehouse. I damn near wanna drop you off at the crib, but I know you ain't tryna hear that shit," I said to her. As much as I loved seeing this side of Janae, I didn't want to expose her to what's about to go down. I don't think she's mentally or emotionally ready for what can happen. This kind of shit can haunt you forever.

"You ain't dropping me off nowhere. You don't understand the situation," she said to me.

"I ain't no dumb ass nigga. I know what the fuck is going on. I can understand you wanting to whoop her ass for continuously trying to fuck with me, but bae, you can beat her ass at any time. This shit is deeper than that," I told her, and I noticed her roll her eyes.

"It ain't just about that bitch Kai. It's deeper than that shit for me too," she said, and I glanced over at her, confused by what she had just said. What the fuck is that supposed to mean?

"What does that mean?" I asked, and she ignored me. "Nae, I know you hear me talking to you. What you mean it's deeper for you too? What the fuck is going on?" I asked her raising my voice. She was acting weird as fuck and I didn't like that shit. She continued to ignore me, so I left the conversation alone for now, but best believe we would be exchanging words once we got back to the crib.

Finally, we pulled up to this abandoned looking warehouse in the middle of nowhere. I picked this place because I knew that it would be the farthest thing from the law's mind. Nobody would even think twice about the outside appearance of this place. About 3-4 black trucks were parked outside, so I knew that my team was already here with the girls. I used this spot whenever one of my people were injured or if I needed to stash somebody and pump them for information, like now.

On one side of the warehouse were a few little rooms that were set up like hospital rooms and the other side is what I called the hell hole. I've lost count of how many bodies this building was responsible for. Most times, if a nigga, or a bitch, was ever brought here, they never made it back home. Motherfuckers talk too much, so I always had to cover my ass, by any means necessary. We walked down a small hallway and entered what I called the holding room. It kind of looked like a police interrogation room, which was ironic to me. Motherfuckers always thought they were really at the police station about to get questioned, until they saw me. I loved having that kind of power over somebody. That mind control shit is a motherfucker. Once we entered the room, I turned around and looked at Janae who looked terrified.

"You good?" I asked her. Her eyes stayed trained on the third girl for a moment before she looked at me and nodded her head. I looked at her suspiciously but then turned around so that I could get to business. I looked at the three females in front of me and smirked.

"I'm not about to be pussy footing around the questions that I need answers to, so I'mma tell y'all like this...lie to me and I'm shooting you. That's just what it is. So make the right decision when answering these questions. You got me?" I asked and they all nodded their head in fear. I smiled. "Good girls. Now, first things first, how y'all hoes know each other?" I asked, and no one spoke up. I gave them a few more seconds, and still, nobody said a word. I pulled my gun out and took the safety off. These bitches wanted to play with me and I really didn't have the time or energy to be playing games. Lauren finally broke her silence.

"Okay Kai! Okay! We all met through..." she started, but was cut off by Tammy and Chris entering the room.

"Tasha?" Tammy and Chris said simultaneously and then looked at each other suspiciously. "How do you know her?" they said in unison. I looked at Janae who was looking just as confused as I was. This shit was getting weirder by the minute.

31

TAMMY

*a*s soon as I said that last sentence, it dawned on me who Tasha was to him. I chuckled to keep from slapping the shit out of this nigga. I knew this shit wasn't some coincidence. I asked this bitch just a few weeks ago about this nigga and she played it off like all he did was sell her a car. I should've whooped her ass right then and there like I wanted to, but I was being professional. After all, she was my patient. All the shit this scandalous bitch told me about her husband and her past life. I wonder who the fuck else she knew that I knew.

"So, THIS is Tasha? Wow. I just think it's funny how I just asked you how you knew Chris when you were sitting in my office crying yo weak ass eyes out about your husband and you made it seem like it was strictly a business relationship between you and my man. *Oh, he just sold me a car,*" I said mocking the sound of her voice.

"Wait a minute, this bitch is one of your patients?" Janae asked, and I shook my head to say yes, never taking my eyes off of her. "Damn man, how many fucking lives are you going to ruin?" Janae yelled, and I looked at her to see who she was talking to. I know she couldn't have been talking to me. I looked over at her and found her eyes locked on Tasha, which brought numerous questions to my mind.

"How you know who the fuck she is Nae?" Kai'Juan spoke up. I damn near forgot this nigga was even in the room. He was standing off in the corner not saying a fucking word after Chris and I walked into the room.

"Unfortunately, she's my cousin," Janae said, and I looked at her like she was crazy.

"What the fuck you mean she yo cousin? Like, she's your aunt's kid or like your play cousin?" I asked her for clarity.

"Like she's my Daddy's niece," she said rolling her eyes. I shook my head in disgust.

"You gotta be fucking kidding me!" Kai'Juan yelled. Suddenly, Tasha started laughing.

"Y'all are so fucking pathetic," she said like the scene before her was the funniest thing she'd ever encountered. Her laugh only pissed me off more, and before I knew it I was raining blow after blow on her. I was kind of being a weak bitch for beating her ass while she was tied up and couldn't defend herself. But fuck it, she wanted to have all that mouth, she could take this L.

"Tammy, chill out!" I heard Chris yell out to me, but I didn't give a fuck. All these bitches could catch it at this point.

"Oh, so you defending this bitch? Huh?" I yelled at him, still raining blows on Tasha. I've never felt so much rage. After a few more blows, Chris pulled me off of her. Kai'Juan walked over and lifted her chair back up. This bitch had a smile on her face. A bloody smile, but a smile nonetheless. Lauren was sitting next to her crying silently and Imani looked completely unbothered by the entire thing. Crazy ass bitch.

"I'm not defending her T, but if you keep beating on her, you gone kill her," he stated.

"You know what? I'm sick of this shit. You two motherfuckers can have each other. You been running around with this bitch for who knows how fucking long, so obviously you like her. This bitch..." I said pointing to Lauren, "been fucking with Kai and done turned into a stalker and this backstabbing hoe..." I said making eye contact with Imani "done came back from the dead. So, let me just ask the million-dollar question. How do y'all know each other?" I asked with my hand on my hip. Lauren kept looking at Imani and Tasha like they were supposed to save her, and I rolled my eyes. This bitch was so weak.

"Bitch you can talk! You have all that mouth any other time! Speak the fuck up!" Janae yelled at Lauren, who instantly started sobbing loudly. I noticed Imani roll her eyes and Tasha looked disgusted with the both of them.

"You know what? Fuck it! I didn't want to do none of this shit anyway. I don't even like you bitches. We know each other because of Brandon," Tasha said and shrugged her shoulders.

"What? Man, hell naw. That don't even make sense," Kai'Juan said, pulling out his phone. "Yo, B, get to the warehouse right fucking now bro," Kai'Juan said sternly and then hung up the phone. He started to pace back and forth until finally he left out of the room. A few seconds later, a young-looking dude came in and stood in the corner that Kai'Juan was previously standing. Kai'Juan entered the room and let us know that the dude in the corner was going to watch over Imani, Tasha and Lauren while he spoke with us in private. Janae, Chris and I walked out of the room and followed Kai'Juan to the middle of the empty warehouse. Once we stopped walking, Chris was the first to speak up.

"You think what she said is true? We know how Imani is tied to Brandon but how would he know Tasha and Lauren?" he asked us. I shrugged my shoulders. I was so confused right now, and my head was pounding. I really just wanted to go home and get in the bed. Plus, I'm hungry as hell and I have to pee. I'm over being pregnant already.

"I don't know but we about to find out. I can't even say I'd be surprised though. To be honest, Lauren is the only one I'm confused about. I don't see how she would fit into whatever the fuck is going on; but Imani and Tasha make sense. Think about it...we haven't seen Brandon or Imani in forever now all of a sudden Brandon wants to do

32

BRANDON

$\mathcal{I}$ don't know what the fuck Kai'Juan called me for, but I figured some niggas had fucked up and he wanted me to handle it. Imagine my surprise when I walk in and see his bitch, Tammy and bitch ass Chris. Why they were here is beyond me, but I guess I was about to find out.

"My nigga, I need you to fill me in on some shit. Follow me," Kai'Juan said heading towards the interrogation room. We entered the room and I instantly became pissed off. How the fuck did all three of these bitches get caught? Now my plan was fucked. I tried to act like I didn't know who these bitches were, but I'm pretty sure Kai's observant ass picked up on it.

"That one says they all know each other because of you. Is that true?" he asked, eyeing me suspiciously. I stood there for a minute looking at these hoes. At this point it was my life or theirs. Shit, it was probably both of our lives either way it goes. This nigga had all his best soldiers behind him right now, so I know he wasn't on no bull-shit. Somebody wasn't leaving this bitch tonight, if not all of us.

"You takin' the word of some bitches you don't even know?" I asked, trying to save face.

"Nigga that's why I just asked you! Stop acting like a little bitch and answer the fucking question nigga! You and these hoes just randomly pop up from fucking nowhere around the same time and you expect me not to be suspicious when one of them says your name?" he shouted, and I frowned.

"Who the fuck you talkin' to bro? Yo, I understand you confused and shit, but you really need to watch yo fuckin' mouth. You talkin' to me like I'm a bitch and I'mma let you know right now, it ain't no hoe in my blood," I said sternly.

"Answer the fucking question B," he stated in a nonchalant tone. I blew out a frustrated sigh and rubbed my hand over my face. *Fuck it,* I thought. I looked around and noticed Tammy, Chris and Janae standing in the doorway. As bad as I wanted Tammy back, I knew what I was about to say would ruin any chance that I had with her.

"Yeah, bro. I know all three of em. Obviously, Imani is my hoe ass baby moms. I don't think I need to explain that. I met Tasha almost right after I left. I went to ATL to get my mind right and I was kind of trying to build something with Imani, but she took the fuck off. After that, I met Tasha and I was feeling her until I found out what she was really about. The bitch is scandalous Kai. I don't know if you already know this, but her and Janae are cousins. She was fucking Janae's Daddy and then set him up to get knocked for rape. That's not even the half of it. Turns out, she had a baby by the nigga and gave her up for adoption. Ain't no telling where that baby is now. Tasha was my baby though. Despite how fucked up she was towards her own people, I wanted to help her. She helped me raise Asia, and shit, she still is helping me raise her. I loved her because she was down for me and showed me loyalty. She did everything that I thought Imani would of for a nigga plus more. Hell, I even went so far as to marry her. That's how much I loved her ass," I said and looked at Tasha. Once upon a time, I really did love her ass. I stared for a few more moments and finally realized that her face was fucked up. I chuckled to myself because I knew Tammy had gotten to her.

"You married to this bitch?" I heard Tammy yell behind me. I hung my head before turning around to face her. WHAP! I instantly felt a burning sensation on my cheek. Tammy had slapped the shit out of me.

"So, all of that asking if I knew what Tasha looked like when I was telling you about her and Chris was to save your own ass? After all this time, I would've thought you matured but you're still the same nigga. All you really give a fuck about is yourself," Tammy said and then walked away. I turned around to face Kai'Juan. I just know this nigga had something to say.

"Alright so you married the bitch, but that's still not explaining how you know Lauren and why the fuck you're here and what your plan is. I know yo ass got a plan," he said.

"You right, I do have a plan. Tasha ended up putting two and two together and found out that Imani and Tammy used to be friends. She did some digging and realized that Tammy is also friends with Janae. It was originally Tasha's idea to come back, just to piss Janae off, but I had a better idea. I know one thing you can't resist is a fine, thick ass broad, so I recruited Lauren. She was a stripper that worked down in ATL, and I visited her club from time to time. I knew for the right price she'd basically do anything, so I sent her down here first to get close to you, and, well, the rest is history. I came across a problem when she started to really catch feelings for you, so I had to think of something else. That's where Tasha came in. I originally wanted her to come and fuck with you, but by the time she came in the picture you were on your *do the right thing* shit with Janae, so she went to the next best thing," I explained looking at Chris.

"Chris was actually an easy ass target. I thought it would be hard because he was always so fucking loyal to Tammy, but it was just my luck that they were having problems. It was a bonus when Tasha found out that Tammy was a therapist and became her patient. That shit wasn't a part of the plan though. I really think Tash just needed somebody to talk to. Me coming back was always supposed to happen. I really wasn't on no slick shit with you at first. I just wanted to make some money with my bro, but you acted like I was beneath you. Even though I was supplying you with everything, you still acted like I was the worker. What type of shit is that? You always been on that alpha shit since we were little niggas and I always wanted to beat your ass for it. But I thought, fuck it, I'll just take your whole operation and show him who's really boss. I coulda just stopped supplying you, but that was too easy. Plus, I wasn't about to stop my own cash flow just to teach yo bitch ass a lesson," I said smirking.

"Bitch? Nigga if anything, you the bitch. Look at all this shit you doing over a female! Then you wanna turn your back on me and try to set me up because of the way a nigga move? You a weak ass nigga B. On God you are, and I'm through with this entire conversation. Damani, untie these hoes and get them the fuck out of here. I don't want to see you bitches ever again. I should kill every single one of you. The only reason I'm not is because Asia still has to have some type of family in this world. Get all your shit and don't come back. Matter of fact take y'all asses to another country. If you ever set foot back in the United States, I'll kill you. Understood?"

"Nigga fuck no! You must got shit twisted. I ain't gotta do shit just because..." Imani started, but a bullet in between her eyes silenced her for good.

"That bitch always had too much fucking mouth," Tammy said from the door, shocking the shit out of me. Where the fuck did she learn to shoot?

"What the fuck!" Kai'Juan and Chris shouted simultaneously. Tammy shrugged and pointed the gun at Tasha who instantly started to break down. Tammy didn't give a fuck though as she let off two shots into Tasha's chest. POW! POW!

"T chill out!" Kai'Juan yelled and she gave him a look that said, 'shut the fuck up'. I ain't never seen her like this before and I was wondering who the fuck taught her this shit. I know damn well it wasn't Chris. We were all looking at her like she lost her fucking mind. Tammy then pointed the gun towards me. I held my hands up in surrender.

"Tam you really need to chill the fuck out. I ain't ya enemy," I said to her. She cocked her head a little to the left and gave me a look that was hard to read. I really think this girl was losing her damn mind by the second. She had a deranged look in her eyes that I've never seen. I can't even lie, I was scared as fuck.

"You hurt me for the last fucking time Brandon. When you disappeared, I was heartbroken, but I got through it because of Chris and my sister. I fell in love again and I created a life with Chris. Who gives a fuck what we were going through when you decided to come fuck up our lives? That's what couples do. But stupid me, I was so stuck on wanting to live this fucking fairy tale life that I fell right into your trap and fucked up the best thing that happened to me. All for what? For this fake ass friendship that you rebuilt with me? Nigga fuck you. You ain't shit, never was shit, and ain't never gone be shit. I really wished you woulda stayed where the fuck you were at, because you'd still be breathing," she said. The next thing I know, I was on the ground with my chests burning like a motherfucker.

"I'm....sorry...T," I said as I grabbed my chest to try and stop the bleeding.

"Yeah, me too," Tammy said, and then everything went black.

33

LAUREN

"*A*aah!" I screamed as Tammy let off another shot into Brandon's chest. This bitch was crazy as hell and I just knew I was next. Tears streamed down my face as I realized I was living in my last few moments of life. I swear if I could turn back time, I never would have accepted Brandon's offer to come up here. I would've stayed my ass down south where I belonged. If I would've kept it moving like my mind was telling me to, this would have never happened. I would have never met and fell in love with Kai'Juan and I wouldn't be sucked into this bullshit. I had to do or say something if I wanted to live, but what could I possibly do that could change my current situation?

I watched as Tammy looked over his body for a few seconds. Kai shook his head and then ordered the dude that was still standing in the corner to call the "clean-up crew" whatever that means. The dude in the corner nodded his head and then left out of the room. Chris walked over to Tammy, took the gun out of her hand and lightly stroked her face.

"Baby are you ok?" he asked her in the most concerned and loving voice that I'd ever heard. Tammy didn't know how lucky she really was. I'd kill to have a man love me the way he loves her. That type of unconditional love is rare. They stared in each other's eyes for a few moments until Tammy placed her head on his shoulder and started to cry. He rubbed her back to console her and then ushered her out of the room. The only people still in the room with me were Kai'Juan and Janae.

"So, what are we going to do about her?" Janae said pointing at me. Kai'Juan looked at me and ran his hand down his face. He was so handsome, especially when he was frustrated or in deep thought. Regardless of the way this was supposed to play out, I did love him. I know I couldn't have him, especially since he all of a sudden wanted to do the right thing, but that couldn't stop the way I felt about him.

"I really forgot all about this bitch," Kai'Juan said and I frowned.

"Bitch?" I asked for clarification.

"Bitch you heard him! Don't act like you have morals and shit now. You ain't nothing but a stripper who was looking for a come up and now look where that shit got you? All because you wanted to chase after some dick that didn't belong to you. What the fuck did Brandon promise you Lauren? Money? Drugs? Dick? You look like the type of bitch that would do some scandalous shit for some dick. Or are you just plain old stupid? Speak the fuck up when somebody talking to you!" Janae yelled getting in my face.

"You acting real hard now that I'm tied up. Get yo weak ass out my face bitch. You ain't cut like that, stop tryna front for your nigga," I said confidently. This bitch didn't put no fear in my heart. I may have looked and played the part of a weak, timid bitch, but it ain't never been no hoe in me. Ever. I thought she would have learned that after that night in the club.

Janae smirked and walked to the back of my chair and began untying me. "You said one thing right: MY nigga. I'm about to untie you and give you a proper ass whoopin. Bae, you can leave the room. I just need five minutes alone with this hoe. I promise. You can time me," she said glancing up at Kai'Juan.

"Man, I ain't bouta stand outside and let you fight this girl. She already know what it is. Plus, I got something much worse in store for her. Tie her back up Nae and come on," he said winking at me. I'm not sure if that wink was a good or a bad thing, but if it meant me being alone with Kai, then I was with it. Janae let out a frustrated sigh, tied me back up and left out of the room with Kai'Juan following behind her. I let out a sigh of relief, but my temporary relief was quickly replaced with fear. What the hell did he have in store for me?

34

CHRIS

*T*he whole ride home I kept glancing at Tammy to make sure she was okay. I was concerned about her mental and emotional state. I know she ain't never killed nobody, shit, I haven't either, but at the same time, she did that shit so effortlessly. Clean shots and all. I still want to know where the fuck she learned how to handle a gun like that, but I wasn't going to bring it up.

"I can't believe I did that," Tammy said in a barely audible voice. If the radio was on, I wouldn't have been able to hear her. I grabbed her hand and brought it to my lips.

"It's okay baby. You did what you felt you had to do," I said in a reassuring tone. I heard her sniffling and knew she was crying again.

"I left Asia without any parents Chris. Who's going to explain to a 3-year-old that her Mommy and Daddy were never coming back? Oh my God!" she said breaking down. I pulled the truck over, got out and went around to the passenger's side. I yanked the door open and told Tammy to hop out of the car. Surprisingly, she didn't object.

"Just let it out right now bae. I can't imagine how you must be feeling right now, but it will get better over time. I promise you T. Just let it out right now and everything else we will work through together. I got you," I told her. She grabbed my hands and then let out a blood curdling scream and then broke down. I couldn't help but to cry with her. We stayed standing on the side of the road, crying for a few minutes before she pulled away.

"I love you and I'm so sorry. I'm sorry for everything," she said, and I kissed her forehead.

"Don't even worry about it. It's ok. Let's go home, ok?" I said, and she nodded in response.

We made it home about 45 minutes later and Tammy told me she was going upstairs to take a hot bath. I went into the living room and sat on the couch, confused. It's crazy how everything could go from damn near perfect to all fucked up. I can't believe Tasha and Brandon were married. I never even knew she had a husband. This shit was really crazy. Then on top of that, she was related to Janae. Janae claimed that she couldn't stand Tasha, but how do we know that she isn't in on this whole plan? Speaking of this "plan", it still didn't make sense. Brandon thought of all this shit just to win Tammy over? If you ask me, his ass needed to be in a mental hospital some fucking where. Who thinks like that?

I sat on the couch for a few more minutes and then decided to go upstairs and get in the bed. When I reached the top of the stairs, I could hear Tammy talking on the phone. Against my better judgement, I stood at the top of the stairs and eavesdropped.

"Nay, he was married to the bitch that Chris was fucking with," Tammy stated, clearly on the phone with her sister. I know she had to be pissed off. "I just don't understand why the nigga did all of this just to win over some territory and me. It ain't never been that deep. I wish he would've stayed where the fuck he was. I almost feel bad for killing his ass because I never got any closure. I Just acted strictly off of impulse. But fuck it, it is what it is. Then for Janae to be Tasha's cousin has me questioning if I should even trust Janae anymore, and she's the closest thing to me besides you and Chris. I don't know Nay. I'm just confused and I'm over it. I don't need to be stressed out carrying this baby, you know?" she rambled, and I decided to let her vent to her sister.

I went out to the backyard and sat in one of the chairs on the patio. I'd stopped smoking years ago, but times like this, I needed a blunt badly. I quickly went back into the house and retrieved a blunt from my man cave. Yes, I had a few already rolled. Shit, you never know. After sparking up the blunt and taking a few hits I began to feel a little more relaxed. A few minutes passed before Tammy came out on the patio with me.

"Damn, you that stressed, huh?" she asked with a slight chuckle. I looked up at her and shrugged my shoulders.

"Yeah, I guess I am. I hate that shit had to go down like this T. I hate that all of this bullshit started because I kept a secret from you. I should've just been real with you and let you know what was going on with my job and shit. But that's in the past bae, and I want to let you know that I really am working on being a better man. That shit with Tasha was a mistake. And before you ask, no, we never fucked. I admit, I was really starting to like her, but only because it seemed like she was giving me everything that you weren't at the time. Plus, I felt like you were pushing me away, so I didn't know what else to do. She was my confidant when I was vulnerable, and I see now she took advantage of that and used it for her own malicious reasons. I never meant to hurt you T. I love you, and I'm still in love with you. That ain't never going to change. Ever. Especially now since we're about to start a family. I just want to be able to work past this together, as a team. No more secrets and better communication. That's all we need bae. So, I'm going to say this again, are you in this 100%? Are you willing to make this work?" I asked looking into her eyes. I wanted her to know that I was dead ass serious. Tammy was it for me and I really felt fucked up about the way things had been going these pasts few months. I wanted Tammy to be my wife and put a few more babies in her.

Tammy looked at me with a blank expression for a few moments and then a smile spread across her face. "Yes, we can make it work baby," she said and then walked over to me and sat on my lap. She straddled me and then kissed me passionately and I knew that everything would be ok.

35

KAI'JUAN

I left the warehouse and dropped Janae off at the crib, just because I didn't want her to see what was about to go down with Lauren. Honestly, I didn't know what the fuck I was going to do with her ass, and I didn't want Janae to know that. She would cuss me out and probably try to kill me. It might sound fucked up to say, but I really didn't want to hurt that girl. Even with knowing that she was in cahoots with the devil, it was just something that was telling me she was just an innocent bystander. Shit, the way it was explained, she ain't know what the fuck she was getting herself into. Imani and Tasha had an ulterior motive, but Lauren was just trying to make some extra cash, which in a way I could understand.

After dropping off Janae I headed back to the warehouse, noticing that my soldiers were still on guard. That's what the fuck I liked to see. A team that did what the fuck I said. Niggas these days were hard headed as fuck and did whatever the fuck they wanted to do. Walking into the room that Lauren was being held in, I noticed that she had fallen asleep sitting in the chair. As fucked up as this may sounded, I couldn't say that I didn't have any type of feelings for her. She was a cool ass female that just so happened to fall in love with the wrong nigga. I can admit I lead her on, filled her head with dreams that I knew were never going to fucking happen, but I can't say that I don't care about her. I gave a fuck if she lived or died and that was fucking with me.

I banged on the table a couple of times to wake her up. She instantly shot up, shocked by the unexpected noise. Once she realized where she was and what was going on, she started to cry.

"Kai, please don't kill me. I'm sorry. I never meant for none of this to happen," she said through her sobs. I looked at her for a moment and then ran my hand over my face. I always did that shit when I was confused or stressed out. In this case, I was both. I leaned over the steel table and just looked at her.

"When you found yourself catching feelings, why the fuck didn't you end it and just walk away? You knew what type of nigga I was, and yet, you stayed the fuck around and played yourself. Why?" I asked with a serious expression on my face. I wanted her to know that I could and would end her life if she tried any slick shit.

"I tried but it was too late! I even went as far as purchasing a ticket back to Atlanta. I made it all the way to the airport before Brandon caught up with me and threatened to kill me if I didn't follow through with the plan. As much as he tried to act like he was still your brother, he hated and envied you. I really don't know why. Brandon was sick in the head, but I allowed him to play with my brain and my life. That probably makes me a dumb bitch, but once I started falling in love with you, I wanted to stay for my own reasons. I wanted you to myself, and I know that at some point you wanted me too. Be honest with yourself Kai. I wasn't in this by myself. Side chick or not, you had some kind of feelings for me," she said looking me dead in my eye.

That shit made me feel some type of way. I left out of the room without saying another word and just stood in the big open space, trying to get my mind right. My phone vibrated in my pocket and I sighed because I already knew who it was.

"Yeah bae?" I said answering the phone.

"Everything good?" she asked in a concerned tone. I wanted to tell her the truth, since I was trying to be this new nigga and shit. I wanted to let her know that I didn't think I could go through with this shit, but I didn't feel like hearing her fucking mouth. So, I did what any nigga would do, I lied.

"Yeah, everything is straight. I'll be home in a minute," I said. We said our goodbyes and I headed back into the room. Fuck it, I had to do what I felt was best.

"I'mma let you in on something Lauren. You might be right. I did have some type of feelings for you, but when I decided that I wanted to do right by my girl, I meant that shit. I wish you would've just bowed out gracefully," I said shaking my head.

"Kai please don't hurt me. Please. I promise if you let me go, I'll disappear. I'll even leave the country if you want me to. I'm begging you. Please!" she yelled, pleading for her life. All this yelling and crying was pissing me the fuck off. Off impulse, I charged towards her side of the table and put my hands around her throat. I didn't give a fuck that she was tied up to the chair and she couldn't even attempt to defend herself.

"I never let nobody get close to me and the one time I do, I let in a snake ass bitch like you. I could kill you right now!" I said in a harsh whisper. I looked into her brown eyes and noticed that her eyes were starting to roll in the back of his head. Suddenly, I let go and she started grasping for air. "If I ever see you again, you're dead. Do you fucking understand?" I asked, and she nodded her head. I walked out of the room and headed towards my car. I pray to God that Janae or nobody else found out that I let Lauren go. If they did, it would be hell to fucking pay.

36

TAMMY

*S*ix *Months Later*

"Bae come on before you make us late!" I yelled up the stairs. You would think since I was eight months pregnant that I'd be the one taking all day. It can't possibly take that long for a nigga to shower and put on a shirt, pants and shoes. We were headed to my doctor's appointment. At this point in my pregnancy, I was going to see the doctor every couple of weeks. I had gestational diabetes, which is the type of diabetes that develops during pregnancy. I causes high blood sugar that can affect my pregnancy and my baby's health. Hopefully, after I deliver the baby, that'll be the end of it, but my doctor told me that I am at risk for type two. So far, I've been controlling it really well by eating healthy foods (most times) and exercising two to three times a week.

Chris has been amazing throughout this whole process. He's been catering to my every need, and I've been eating it up. I loved that he was in love with the thought of becoming a father. We've reconnected over the months and I couldn't be more thankful.

Finally, Chris came down the steps dressed casually in a pair of jeans, a long-sleeved black t-shirt and black Timberland boots. I couldn't lie, my man was fine as hell. He did something to me when he wore black, and he knew it.

"You look like a whole meal," I said eyeing him seductively. He smirked at me and then kissed my lips.

"Don't start no shit T. We already running late," he reminded me. I playfully rolled my eyes.

"It's your fault. Now come on so I can come back home and lay on the couch," I said, and he laughed.

"You lazy as hell," he said leading the way to the car. I shrugged my shoulders.

"I'm eight months pregnant, big as a whale, and on maternity leave. I have the right to be lazy," I responded. He lifted his hands up in mock surrender.

"My bad big mama," he said opening the car door for me and I punched him in the arm. He knew I hated being called that shit. He laughed as he closed the door and walked to the driver side. On the drive to the doctor's office, we joked and listened to music. It felt good to be carefree again. We were finally moving past all the bullshit and I prayed it stayed like that. About fifteen minutes later, we arrived at my OB/GYN. Chris helped me out of the car and led me into the office. It took no time for us to be escorted into a room.

"What do you think they're going to say?" Chris asked. I looked at him and shrugged my shoulders. We were here today because the baby had not gone into position for labor, meaning that he wasn't head down. Usually a baby turns at about 34 weeks. I was currently 36 weeks and still he hadn't turned head down. At this point, he was breeched. Yes, I said he. Our little baby boy was being born soon and we still hadn't decided on a name for him. I wanted to just call him CJ (Chris Jr) and call it a day, but Chris was being difficult. What kind of man didn't want a junior?

"I'm not sure, but I hope they say he's turned. I really don't want to have any complications. I just want him to be happy and healthy, you know?" I said to Chris and he nodded his head.

"He will be bae, don't even trip," Chris responded. "Do you want to take maternity pictures? We probably should've talked about this a few months ago, but since he's so close to being here, don't you think we should capture the moment?" he asked. I had honestly never thought about doing anything special like that, but the fact that he did made me smile.

"That'll be nice babe, and it'll give me a reason to get fine," I said and we both chuckled. I was always down for anything that required me to get dolled up. We chit chatted for a few until the doctor knocked on the door. I smiled as Dr. Worthy entered the room. Something about her always made me feel welcomed and safe. I knew she had my best interest at heart.

"How are you doing today Tammy? Chris?" she greeted.

"Fine," we both said in unison. She washed her hands and then came over to the table where I was laying.

"Let's go ahead and check on this baby boy, shall we?" she said lifting up my shirt and putting the gel on my stomach. She grabbed the transducer and began going over my belly, trying to see what position our baby was in. I said a silent prayer that my baby would be okay.

"Good news!" Dr. Worthy said after a few minutes. "It looks like he is starting to turn. He's not completely head down yet; he's kind of sideways, but he's moving in the right direction. We can check back in another week to see his position," she said, and I let out a sigh of relief.

"Thank God!" I said.

"Yes, this is great news. In the meantime, let's put you on the monitor to check the pace of his heart and get your vitals. After that, we'll be all done, and I'll see you in a week," she said, and I nodded my head in agreement. The entire process took about 30 minutes and then we were out the door.

"I'm glad he's starting to change positions. I'm kind of scared of C-Sections," I said to Chris as we got back in the car.

"Why are you scared?" he asked.

"I just don't like surgery and I want to avoid it in any way possible," I stated. I didn't want to admit that I'd had an abortion a year ago. Chris would probably kill me. I just wasn't ready at the time.

Although we were happy and financially stable, I wasn't emotionally or mentally ready to care for another human being.

"I get that. Kind of like the same way people are afraid of needles. It makes sense," he said pulling off. "You hungry? We can stop and get some lunch, or we can just head to the house," he asked.

"I'm always hungry," I said, and he laughed.

"Yeah, you are. I was about to say fat ass, but I can't have you trying to swing on me while I'm driving," he said and we both laughed. We ended up having lunch at my favorite Coney Island spot. Lately, all I've been wanting is greasy food. Chicken, cheese fries, pizza, burgers, milkshakes. Basically, everything that I wasn't supposed to eat, but I balanced it out well. I set aside the weekends for my days to pig out and on the week days, I followed a strict diet due to my diabetes. Today would have to be a cheat day. I deserved it. While we sat and ate, I couldn't help but to feel like I was being watched. I kept looking around to see if I noticed anything or anybody that could be suspicious, but nothing looked out of the ordinary.

"Bae, you good?" Chris asked me giving me a weird look.

"Yeah I'm good. I just have a weird feeling," I stated.

"What kind of feeling?"

"Like I'm being watched or some shit. But don't worry about it, I could be trippin," I said shrugging it off. I could tell Chris wanted to ask more questions, but he didn't, which I was grateful for. We finished our meal and headed home to relax. As much as I wanted to, I just couldn't shake the feeling that somebody was watching me. I kept telling myself that the baby had my mind messed up, but my gut was telling me it was more than that.

37

CHRIS

*T*oday was the day that we were going to take maternity pictures. I was excited for the simple fact that Tammy was huge, and she had this pregnant glow that I know would look even better in pictures. In the past few weeks, I can tell that something has been on her mind heavily, but I figured when she was ready, she would share whatever it was. I didn't want to pressure her, but I didn't want her to keep things bottled up either.

That's part of the reason why I mentioned the maternity shoot. I thought that it would loosen her up and make her feel a little more at ease. Shit, we've been through some crazy shit this past year, and we never really talked about it. I thought that after the incident at the warehouse, Tammy would want to talk about it, but she didn't. After she had that breakdown in the car, she acted like nothing ever happened, which concerned me. I know she had to feel some type of way about killing Brandon and Tasha, but I can't force it out of her.

I looked up and saw Tammy walking down the steps looking just as beautiful as the first day that I laid eyes on her. She had on a royal blue maxi dress that had two slits on the side, exposing her thighs when she walked, and her breasts were sitting up just right. Her hair was done in a middle part and curled to perfection and her nails and make up were also done. If she wasn't already pregnant, I'd put another baby in her. I loved that she could do her hair and make-up herself. A few years ago, when Janae was thinking about opening up her beauty bar, I suggested that Tammy do hair and makeup professionally, but she said her heart wasn't in it. I thought it would be a great side hustle, but she said it was just a hobby. Shit, I wish I could do hair and make-up. I'd make a killing off these females. I'd probably make way more money doing that than selling these cars. She smiled as she walked towards me.

"You look beautiful bae," I said and pecked her on the lips.

"Thank you. You over there looking like a whole meal yourself," she said, and I took a step back and posed like a model, which made her laugh. I also had on royal blue: a button up, some black slacks and royal blue dress shoes. I must admit, I was a simple dresser, but I still had the sauce. We walked out of the house and hopped in the car, heading to our photo shoot. Once I hopped on the freeway, I kept seeing this same black Benz behind us. I couldn't see who was behind the wheel because the tint was thick, but I knew when somebody was following me. I looked over at Tammy and saw that she'd fallen asleep, which was good. I didn't want her to know what was going on and then start panicking. I noticed that the car stayed about three cars behind me, trying not to look suspicious, but every turn I made, they did too, but I had something for them. The exit that I was supposed to get off on was coming up, but I decided to go another route and drive in the direction of the nearest police station, which was about four minutes away. After I got off the freeway, I noticed that the car was still behind me, but the driver must've caught on and realized I was heading towards the police station and made a U-Turn. *What the fuck was that about?* I stated turning around and heading towards our destination. I made a mental note to talk to Kai about that shit.

38

KAI'JUAN

"So, you're 100% positive that you want to do this?" Chris asked me. We were in the jewelry store looking at engagement rings. Yeah that's right, I said it, and I don't give a fuck. A nigga was about to settle down and take that step. Shit, I felt like I was married already. We already lived together, I took care of anything financial and she held down anything dealing with the household, along with her own business. My girl was the shit and I still felt fucked up about how I treated her all those years. I look back on that shit and can't believe that I was even that type of nigga, but I guess I just had to get that shit out of my system. That, or I had to face the fact that she would really leave my ass and never come back.

"Hell yeah I'm sure. You know I wouldn't be in this bitch if I wasn't sure. I'm not gonna lie, I'm nervous as fuck Kai. This marriage shit ain't no joke," I said, admitting my fears for the first time. I already had cold feet and I didn't even pop the question yet. This was some real grown man shit. I mean, one woman for the rest of my life. Then, if I do cheat, she can take half my shit. How the fuck was that fair? Like Rick Ross said, "you wasn't with me shooting in the gym!" I know what you're thinking: *nigga, that song is old as fuck,* but fuck you, it's still relevant.

"I'm just making sure nigga. I don't want you changing your mind after you already asked her and then she kills you," Chris laughed. I gave him a playful dirty look.

"I know you ain't talkin. Janae knows better than to try me, but I know T will pop yo ass. I've seen it with my own eyes," I said thinking back to that. I never knew Tammy had it in her to pop off like that, but she handled that situation with no hesitation. She acted like she hated my guts, but I knew deep down I was like a brother to her. That night was definitely a proud brother moment.

"So, have we decided on a specific ring?" the salesman said coming back to the spot that Chris and I have been for the past 10 minutes.

"Yeah, I think the princess cut fits her perfectly. I'll take this one," I said pointing to a ring in the center of the display. It was gorgeous and it fit Janae perfectly. She usually wasn't flashy, but I know she wanted her engagement ring to be extra, but subtle, which matched her personality. I also remember her telling me that if we were to ever get married that she wanted a princess cut engagement ring, that had diamonds all around; so, I got her a 15-carat princess cut diamond ring with diamonds all throughout. She was probably going to pass the fuck out when she saw this ring. It reminded me of Ciara's ring when Future proposed to her. I only remember what it looked like because Janae showed me in the midst of our conversation.

"Great choice! You are aware that this ring is close to $2 million?" the salesman stated, and I gave him a blank expression.

"You are aware that I don't give a fuck? Ring me up and make sure it's a size six. Not a five and not a seven, a six. You got that?" I questioned, and he nodded his head in shock. Racist ass probably thought I didn't have the bread. He shook his head to acknowledge that he understood my request and went to the back to do whatever it is that they do back there.

"Can you believe that motherfucker?" Chris said sounding surprised by the salesman's actions. I shrugged my shoulders in response. I hated to say it, but I was used to that type of shit. You walk into an uppity establishment, and the white people start to look at you like you don't belong. I didn't give a fuck though. The looks didn't bother me, but the blatant disrespect and racism did, which is why I responded the way that I did.

I paid for the ring and we exited the store. Once in my truck, I handed Chris the ring and told him to hide it somewhere safe until it was time for me to pop the question.

"Wouldn't it make more sense to hide it in the safe in your office or something?" Chris asked.

"Hell nah. I only have super important work files and a few stacks in the safe at the dealership. That would be stupid as fuck for me to have any personal important information in that safe. What if we get robbed? God forbid. But shit, it can happen. I would hate for it to happen and I've lost every important piece of information that I have," I stated, and Chris nodded his head letting me know that he agreed. Suddenly, I thought about a better place to hide it and tapped Chris's chest. "Matter of fact let me get that back. We're about to make a stop," I stated heading towards my new destination.

"Man, where we going? I gotta get to the house. I need to set up this nursery before Tammy rips me a new asshole," Chris complained.

"Alright Mr. Mom chill the fuck out. You'll be home in time to do your arts and crafts. This will only take a few minutes. Ole pussy whipped ass," I said, and he just shook his head. A few minutes later we pulled up to Chase bank on 14 Mile and John R. Surprisingly, Chris didn't ask any questions. He simply hopped out of the car and allowed me to lead the way. Once we entered the bank, I went and signed in on a clip board located in the left-hand corner of the room by a window. After signing in, I took a seat and waited for a Personal Banker to come out and assist me. A few minutes later, I heard my name being called. When I looked up, I could have walked right out the bank. Standing before me was Lauren's best friend, Cassie, looking rather professional in her blue Chase blazer and a long black pencil skirt. This bitch had always hated me because she felt like I was stringing her girl along, which I was, but she didn't have proof of that.

"I was hoping that there were two Kai'Juan Morris' in the world, but nope, it's just you," she said faking laughing. I slightly rolled my eyes.

"What's going on Cassie? When did you start working here?" I asked, trying not to sound agitated. I've been to this branch a million times and I've never seen her here. Now, all of a sudden, this is her place of employment.

"I just transferred three months ago from one of the branches in Warren. What are you here for today?" she asked, and I explained that I wanted to get into my safety deposit box. After taking me to her desk and verifying some information she took me down to my safety deposit box. I placed the ring in the box along with the receipt (just in case Janae wanted to be nosy) and locked the safety deposit box. Once that was done, Cassie led me back to the main lobby and Chris and I headed out the door.

"Where do you know her from?" Chris asked looking at me.

"That's Lauren's best friend," I stated, and he nodded his head.

"It kind of seemed like she was feelin' you," Chris said, and I gave him a confused look.

"Cassie? Hell naw. That bitch hates my guts," I said.

"Bitches always say they hate the guy that they really like. It's common female knowledge. They don't want you to know that you like them, so they'll go ask their friend or try to find their social media. Shit, niggas are like that too," he said, and I had to agree with him. I never thought about it like that, but I guess he was right. In this case though, he was way off. If Cassie could, she would kill me and not think twice about it.

I dropped Chris off at home and headed towards my own place. During the drive, I tried to think of romantic ways to propose to Janae. I still can't believe that I'm about to do this shit. I needed to call some of her family and start putting this shit together, but Janae's relationship was so strained with her family, I didn't know who to call.

When I pulled up to the house, I noticed that Janae's car was not in the driveway, which meant that she hadn't made it home yet. I figured she had to still be at work. I walked inside the house and went up to the bedroom so that I could take a shower. I made sure to put my 9mm on the dresser, just in case. Janae hated that I had a gun in the house, but little did she know, I had guns all around this motherfucker, they were just hidden. I never wanted a motherfucker to catch me slippin'. Nobody really knew where we lived, but it was just a safety precaution. You could never be too careful, especially with the shit that I did. Although I stayed lowkey and didn't really get my hands dirty, I know that niggas knew who the fuck I was.

I took a quick shower and then entered the bedroom again, and almost shitted myself looking at the person that was sitting on my bed like they owned that motherfucker.

"Long time no see Kai," Lauren said with a smirk on her face. *Where the fuck did this bitch come from?* I thought I told her that if I ever saw her I would off her ass. I looked over at the dresser and noticed that the gun was gone. *Fuck!* I thought. I didn't want to have to kill this bitch with my bare hands, but I would if I had to.

"Bitch, you got some fucking nerve! What the fuck are you doing here, and in my crib at that?" I said moving towards her. Lauren tried to act hard, but the way that she moved back on the bed let me know that I still scared the shit out of her, which I liked.

"For somebody who doesn't have any power right now, you're talking big shit," she said getting off of the bed and standing up. We were now standing on opposite sides of the bed and I wanted to hop across this bed and choke her, but I had to be smart about this. I couldn't have the place where my girl and I laid our heads become a crime scene. Not only that, I didn't want Janae to know that I let this bitch live. She'd probably kill me. This is exactly why I hated catching feelings for bitches. I should've just let Janae whoop her ass and then kill her, but I had a conscience and shit when it came to her and I fucking hated it. I was starting to turn soft and it was pissing me off.

Against my better judgement, I quickly hopped over the bed and lunged at Lauren, catching her by the throat and pinning her to the wall. The towel that was wrapped around my waist had fallen to the floor, so I was butt ass naked, but I didn't give a fuck. I was going to choke some sense into this bitch.

"I told you if you ever showed your face I would kill you. You must want to die. Is that it?" I said squeezing her throat harder. I looked into her round eyes as she tried to say my name. I loosened my grip just a tad bit so that I could hear her beg for her life. It was something about the desperation in a person's voice that gave me a sick thrill.

"Kai, please," she said with tears streaming down her beautiful round face.

"Please, what?"

"I...came back...for...you," she said struggling to speak. I frowned my face and let go of her throat. I took a step back and looked at her coughing and trying to catch her breath.

"For me? I don't fucking want you! What part of that do you not understand! Whatever you thought we had is dead! You need to get yo crazy ass the fuck out of my house and I'm not gone tell yo ass again. You already got a warning out of me and you didn't follow that shit. For the simple fact that I don't want my crib to become a fucking crime scene, I'm letting you live. GET THE FUCK OUT!" I yelled. I tried to keep my calm, but this shit was just too much. I looked at her still sitting on the floor. She had the nerve to be licking her lips seductively. I followed her eyes to what the fuck she was staring at, which was my flaccid penis. This bitch was really staring at my dick like I hadn't choked the shit out of her just moments before. I went to my dresser and grabbed some underwear to put on. Lauren got off the floor and stood right in front of the dresser.

"I'm gonna leave for now. But just so you know, I'm not leaving Michigan without you. I know you love me. You may think you love her, but I know better. What we had was real, which is why you let me live in the first place. I've been being patient and abided by your rules, but I'm not going anywhere unless you come with me, or we'll both just end up in body bags...together," she said blowing a kiss at me and then walking out of the room. A few moments later I heard the front door close. I sat on the bed and ran my hands over my face. I had to do something about this bitch.

39

TAMMY

*T*wo *Weeks Later*

I was sitting at the house, on the couch, as usual. I'm so tired of being pregnant. I only had two more weeks to go before my due date, but dammit, I wanted this boy out of me. I'd just gone to the doctor the day before yesterday, and my big boy was officially in position for labor. Besides being a fat pregnant lady, I was going through some shit emotionally. I don't know what it was, but I've been thinking about Brandon heavy lately. I know that Chris could tell I've been a little distant, and it wasn't on purpose, my mind was just everywhere. I couldn't tell him that I've been sitting around, sad about the same nigga that I killed. I still can't believe that I killed someone. Shit, two people. People who, at one point, meant everything to me.

I grabbed my MacBook and started to google therapist in my area. My mind kept replaying the day that I killed Brandon and Imani over and over in my head. I had nightmares about it, and I know that I couldn't let this haunt me. It just scares me to know that I am capable of doing some savage shit like that. I tell my own patients about the meanings of their dreams/nightmares. I know that a lot of times, getting shot can mean the dreamer is worried about some kind of confrontation (partner, co-worker, etc.). I just couldn't figure out what the hell these nightmares meant, and I needed a better under-standing before I lost my fucking mind.

"What you over here researching?" I heard Chris ask from behind me, and I damn near jumped out of my skin.

"You scared me!" I said holding my chest. Chris laughed a little and then apologized for startling me.

"My bad bae, I just came down here to see if you wanted to try to walk CJ down again," he stated, and I nodded my head. These past few days, Chris and I have been walking the block three times a day. The doctor told us that sex and exercise helps start the labor process, so we've been fucking like rabbits and walking around our neighbor-hood. I needed this boy to come out of me. I'm so tired of sharing my body. I don't see how women had four and five kids. I'm definitely one and done!

"Yeah we can go ahead and walk. I need to get up from this couch," I stated. Chris came around to help me, and as soon as I stood up, the doorbell rang.

"I got it," Chris said heading towards the front door. A few moments later, Janae entered the living room. "I'm about to go in the room and chill while y'all do whatever it is y'all do," Chris said heading towards his man cave. I nodded my head and then looked at my sister.

"What are you doing here?" I asked, surprised to see her. She had been ducked off lately, which is weird because she usually always let me know where she was and what she was doing.

"Damn, I need a reason to come see my girl?" she asked.

"No, but bitch I haven't really spoken to you these past couple of weeks. Where the hell have you been?" I asked her, and she just shrugged.

"Girl, working, trying to get this money," she said nonchalantly, and I nodded my head. Janae opened her beauty bar a few months ago and things were going extremely well for her. I was proud of my girl. She worked hard to have her own shop.

"Bitch you trying to use the work excuse. I know it's more than that. We usually always talk, work or not. You know what, I was just about to walk around the block, you can come with me and fill me in," I said, and she gave me a look.

"Walk? I came over here to chill with you, not get a workout in," she said, and I rolled my eyes.

"Well you can do both. Now bring ya ass," I said playfully hitting her thigh. She reluctantly got up and I let Chris know that I was going to walk with Janae.

"So, what's going on Nae?" I asked her, and she looked at me with a sad expression on her face. I abruptly stopped walking and looked her in her eyes. She looked like she wanted to cry.

"I think Kai is back to his old self," she said sadly.

"Why do you think that?" I asked.

"It's just a feeling I have. You know they say a woman's intuition is usually right? Every time Kai was cheating on me or hiding something from me, I got this same feeling, but I always ignored it, thinking I was crazy. I know better now. At this point, I'm ready to just walk away. He's being secretive again, changed the code on his phone, he doesn't answer the phone half the time. Granted, he still comes home at a decent hour, but I just feel like things are slowly going back to the way they used to be and I'm not taking that shit no more T," she said, and I nodded my head. I can understand how my girl was feeling. I had the same problems with Brandon when we were together, but my sister always told me that a woman knows when she's had enough, and when she's really ready to just walk away, she will. I wanted to believe that Kai'Juan has changed, because, let's face it, that nigga was a straight asshole a few months ago. I mean, he's still an asshole, but I can tell he's calmed down a lot and he's really been trying to change for Nae. Shit, even my relationship with Kai has gotten better, but I think that's because he's seen how I can get, and he decided he doesn't want those problems, which is smart.

I stretched out my arms and gave Janae a hug. "Why don't you just ask him? I honestly think he is really trying Nae. Don't just write him off. You've been loving him and by his side this long, I think your relationship is worth at least talking about it," I said honestly. "If he is cheating though, we can fuck all his shit up," I said, and she laughed.

"Oh, trust me, if he's cheating, I'm killing him," she said seriously, and I gave her a look. She looked at me and then let out a small gasp.

"My bad T. I ain't mean to..." she started to say, but I stopped her.

"Don't worry about it. I'm good," I lied, and we started to walk again. During the walk, I kept feeling what I thought could be contractions, but my doctor told me that they could just be Braxton hicks contractions, so I didn't worry about it too much. We walked for about thirty minutes until I started to get tired. We made it back to the driveway and started walking towards the front door when Janae stopped me.

"Bitch did you pee on yourself?" she asked looking at the driveway. I looked down and notice a wet trail that lead right to where I was standing. I looked down at my feet and that's when I noticed that my leggings were soaking wet.

"Oh shit! I think my water broke!" I shouted, and Janae's eyes widened.

"CHRIS! CHRIS!" we both shouted in unison. Janae ran to the front door screaming his name. After what felt like 5 minutes, they both came running out of the house. Chris had my hospital bag in his hand. Surprisingly, he looked calm.

"Oh, shit it's really happening!" he said excitedly. "Come on baby, let's get in the car," he stated guiding me towards the car. I was just about to sit down in the seat when I felt an excruciating pain surge throughout my stomach and pelvis area.

"Aaaarrrrrggggghhhh!" I screamed. It felt like somebody was twisting my stomach and beating on it with a hammer at the same time. "GET ME TO THE FUCKING HOSPITAL NOW!" I yelled and Chris damn near pushed me in the car. Janae hopped in the back and Chris ran to the driver's side door. I didn't even bother to put my seatbelt on as Chris sped out of the driveway and down the street. Thankfully, we didn't live too far from the hospital. Chris drove like a bat out of hell, passing red lights and almost crashing into other cars. The pain in my stomach subsided for a moment and I remembered to pace my breathing like the doctor instructed me during my last visit.

"I said get me to the hospital, not fucking kill me!" I shouted at Chris and he ignored me as he continued to speed through traffic. About five minutes later, we pulled up to the emergency wing of the hospital. Janae was the first to hop out and run into the entrance of the hospital to get help. Chris came around to my side and tried to help me get out of the car. I thought that I would be able to walk into the hospital, but as soon as both legs were firmly on the ground, I felt weak. "I can't do it Chris! I need a wheelchair!" I said with tears coming down my eyes. It felt like my stomach and my vagina were going to fall out at any minute. Janae came out of the emergency entrance with what looked like a nurse, a security guard and a wheel chair behind her. They placed me in the wheelchair and then wheeled me into the hospital. I was immediately taken up to the maternity ward. I can't lie, I was scared shitless.

Once in the room, they took all my clothes off, put a hospital gown on me and got me into the hospital bed. They hooked me up to a machine that they said monitored the baby's heartrate. Shortly after, Dr. Worthy, my OB/GYN came and examined me, then took a look at my cervix.

"Ok, so I have good news. You're about 6 centimeters dilated and you're also in active labor, so it shouldn't be too long before CJ makes his entrance. We usually like to wait until you're about 8-10 cm dilated to start pushing, but you're well on your way," she stated, and I nodded my head to let her know that I understood.

At least this shit was almost over. I don't think I would survive being in labor too much longer. "I'm going to make my rounds, but I'll be back to check on you shortly. If you need anything, you can just page me or the nurses by using those buttons," Dr. Worthy stated pointing at the two buttons next to the hospital bed. One was labeled Nurse's Station and the other was labeled Doctor. She left out of the room leaving just me, Chris, Janae and the nurse. Janae was on her phone texting away, probably letting Kai'Juan and my sister know that I was in labor.

"Do you need any medicine for the pain Ms. Sinclair?" the nurse asked, and I looked at her like she was stupid.

"Hell yeah! Go get that shit now!" I yelled, and she nodded her head, quickly leaving out of the room. Chris came over and held my hand.

"It's going to be okay baby. Just think, our baby boy is almost here," he stated in a soothing tone. I know that he was just trying to help and make this process a little easier for me, but I just really wanted to slap the shit out of him in this moment. If it hadn't been for him and his little swimmers I wouldn't be going through all this pain. Instead of cussing him out like I wanted to do, I rolled my eyes as another contraction came.

"Ohhhhhh!" I said in agony, squeezing Chris' hand as hard as I could.

"Ah, shit!" I heard him say, like me squeezing his hand was really hurting as bad as this fucking contraction. I loosened the grip that I had on his hand as the contraction subsided one again. I couldn't take this off again on-again shit. Either these contractions were going to hurt, or they weren't. A knock on the door caused us to look up. I noticed the same nurse and a different doctor come in with some tools that I hoped were my damn drugs. I was happy that all the doctors and nurses that I'd encountered were black. I don't know if I really trusted white people with my baby and my vagina. I looked at the doctor again, and he was a rather handsome older man, with salt and pepper hair and milk chocolate skin.

"Ms. Sinclair, my name is Dr. Samuels and I'm the anesthesiologist. I'm here to inject you with epidural. Now, I do want to let you know, that you need to be completely still while I inject the epidural into your spine or it can cause complications. I know that may be hard for you due to the pain of the contractions you're experiencing, but this is a pretty quick process, and, in a few minutes, you won't feel the contractions at all," he stated, and I nodded my head. I'd do anything to make this pain go away. Even if it was just temporary. The doctor instructed me to sit up and then be very still. I caught a glimpse of the needle and almost passed out.

"T, don't trip," Chris said standing in front of me. He knew I was terrified of needles and that motherfucker was huge! Just as the doctor inserted the needle in my spine, I had a contraction. Tears spilled out of my eyes as I tried to muffle my scream and be as still as I could possibly be, but it hurt. I squeezed Chris' hand as I felt the needle go through my spine. The doctor wiped my back and let me know that it was okay to lay back down. As the doctor and nurses left out of the room, my sister entered.

"Aww look at you looking miserable," Anaya joked. I didn't find shit funny. This had to be the worst pain ever.

"Bitch fuck you," I said sticking the middle finger up at her. We sat around and talked and after a few minutes I realized that I hadn't had a contraction.

"Why haven't I felt a contraction? Is it something wrong?" I asked, panicking.

"Tam, they gave you an epidural. You ain't gone feel it right now," Janae said.

"Oh yeah," I said feeling stupid. I laughed a little bit to mask the embarrassment that I felt, and Anaya caught it.

"Girl you don't need to be embarrassed. A whole baby is about to come out of your vagina. We ain't expecting you to be in your right mind right now," she said, and I smiled at her.

"Baby you want some more ice chips?" Chris asked me. I nodded my head and he started to walk out of the room before I stopped him.

"I'm actually starving. Can you get me something to eat?"

"I'll check and see if you can eat anything yet. Dr. Worthy said that they usually don't let you eat until after the baby is born, just in case they have to perform a C-Section," he said, and I sunk down in the bed like a brat. I was going to have to push this big ass baby out on an empty stomach.

A few hours later, Kai'Juan came and cracked jokes with me to take my mind off of being in labor. I was starting to become irritable. I wasn't able to eat anything except ice chips and it was pissing me the fuck off. All I wanted was for my son to enter the world, but he was playing. As of thirty minutes ago, I was dilated at about 7 centimeters and they needed me at 10 centimeters to push. I just wanted him to come the hell on. His time is officially up! Although I was annoyed, I was grateful to have everyone that I loved surrounding me. I thought about my Mom and Dad and wondered if they were looking down on me right now. I missed them so much and it hurt that they would never get a chance to meet their grandson. My parents not being here was the main reason why I didn't have a baby shower. A baby shower was a time to celebrate with your friends and family. The only family that I had left was Anaya and the only friends that I had were Janae and Kai'Juan. They had already showered my baby with gifts and love, so a big extravagant baby shower wasn't needed.

A sharp, excruciating pain entered my body, ripping me from the thoughts of my parents.

"Aaaarrghhhhh!" I screamed out as the contraction progressed. Everybody turned their heads to look at me with concerned expressions on their faces. Chris came over to me and immediately grabbed my hand. He rubbed my head while allowing me to squeeze his hand through the pain. As the contraction subsided, I released my grip on his hand.

"Damn does it hurt that bad?" Anaya had the nerve to ask. If looks could kill, she'd drop dead right now. I wanted to cuss her out, but I decided not to. I needed all of my energy to go towards pushing this baby out. Anaya noticed my dirty look and lifted her hands up in surrender.

"My bad T, shit, I never been pregnant. I don't know how you're feeling," she said, and I just nodded my head. Dr. Worthy came in with a nurse behind him.

"Let's go ahead and check your cervix again," he said, and I nodded my head in agreement. I hope I was able to push because I was over this entire ordeal. I propped my legs up in the stirrups and let Dr. Worthy check me. I felt her fingers at the opening of my vagina, and just as she began to check my cervix, a contraction came. I screamed out in pain again and Dr. Worthy continued to check me.

"I can feel his head. This should be an easy birth Ms. Sinclair. I'm thinking maybe two pushes," he said, and I sighed in relief. She announced that only one visitor could be in the room during delivery, and Kai'Juan, Janae and Anaya politely made their way out of the room, letting me know they would be in the waiting room down the hall. Another nurse walked in and began preparing the incubator for the baby's delivery as Dr. Worthy provided me with the delivery instructions.

"Don't try to push until I tell you to or else you run the risk of tearing and we don't want that. We're going to make this delivery as smooth as possible for you and baby boy. Are you ready?" she asked.

"Hell, yeah I'm ready. Grab my hand Chris," I said holding out my hand for Chris to grab. Once again, he kissed me on my forehead.

"You got this T," he said reassuring me and I smiled. It felt good to have him by my side during all of this. After three pushes, our son, Christopher Lorenzo White Jr was born. He was born at 8 pounds 6 ounces and 21 inches long. He already had full lips like his father and a head full of curly hair like me. I fell in love the moment they placed him in my arms. The nurses went over how to breast feed and swaddle him, and I ate up every minute.

Later that night I watched as Chris, Kai'Juan, Anaya and Janae fell in love with CJ. The nurse came in a few times to let them know that visiting hours were over, but Kai'Juan gave her $200 and told her to mind her business. Leave it up to that nigga to pay off a nurse. After they left, I watched as Chris bonded with CJ. Seeing him interact with our baby made me fall in love all over again. I was truly blessed to have my little family.

40

KAI'JUAN

*A*fter spending a few hours with Chris, Tammy and the baby, I was tired as fuck. Shit, I was so tired you'd think CJ came out of me and not Tam. I can't lie, looking at Janae handle CJ made me want to put a baby in her, but I wanted to make sure this wedding was in place and shit. Do y'all hear me right now? I sound like a fucking sucka, but I guess it wasn't anything wrong with it.

When we got to the house, Janae headed upstairs to shower and get ready for bed and I sat on the couch scrolling through my phone, responding to e-mails, text messages and just looking at my social media timelines. I saw that Lauren had texted me asking me to come meet her tomorrow, but I quickly ignored and deleted the message. I'm trying my hardest to remain on the up and up with Janae. Especially since I had plans on proposing. If she knew that Lauren was alive AND still on some bullshit, she'd lose her fucking mind, and she already wasn't wrapped too tight as it is. I would never say I was scared of a female, but after seeing what Tammy was capable of, Janae ass had me shook; for the simple fact that Janae and Tammy were two peas in a pod.

I stayed on the couch for a while longer until I felt hands caress my shoulders. I grabbed and kissed Janae's hand and watched as she rounded the couch wearing a red corset and a pair of black red bottoms. She smirked at me before going over to the stereo in the corner of the living room and turning on some music. Beyoncé's *Dance for You* played through the speaker as Janae started to dance seductively in front of me. I licked my lips as I watched my girl put on a show for me. After a few minutes she sashayed over to me and straddled me. I grabbed her round ass and squeezed tight, she giggled in response.

"Seeing you with CJ made me horny," she whispered in my ear. It was now my turn to smirk at her. I grabbed her by the back of her neck and pulled her towards me for a kiss. She lightly moaned in my mouth as she sucked on my tongue and kissed me like she really loved a nigga. We kissed for what felt like hours before we finally pulled away.

"Shit, you might get pregnant the way you kissing on a nigga," I said in a serious tone.

"That might not be a bad thing," she said as she pecked my lips and then got off of me.

"I know you not about to leave me like this," I said pointing towards my hard dick.

"Nope, follow me Daddy, I got some shit upstairs for you," she said walking up the steps. I was curious to know what the fuck she had up her sleeve. Walking into the bedroom I saw that Janae had some real special shit set up like it was a nigga birthday. I smiled as I took in all the rose petals on the floor and bed, a bottle of Moet on ice in the center of the bed and a trail of rose petals leading to the bathroom. Walking to the bathroom, I saw Janae sitting at the edge of the tub, waiting for me with a glass of champagne.

"Damn, what's all this for?" I asked her. I looked at the tub and noticed more rose petals in the water along with bubbles. Janae stood up and walked towards me then wrapped her arms around me.

"I just want to let you know that I see how you've changed for me and I really appreciate it Kai. I never ever thought I'd see the sweet, romantic, loving side of you again, but I see it and I'm proud of you. Thank you for putting me first again. Thank you for being loyal and honest, just thank you for wanting to be a better man. Everything that you do doesn't go unnoticed. I love you," she said and kissed me.

"Now, the bath is for me and you. I plan on bathing you and then doing some real nasty things to you," she said and then giggled. I quickly stripped naked and watched as she did the same. I silently cringed at her saying that I've been honest, when I haven't been lately, but I was still going to take full advantage of this night. Shit like this is the reason why I was going to marry her.

* * *

2 *Weeks Later*

Tonight was the night that I was going to pop the question to Janae. It was also her birthday. She'd been so busy with her shop and helping Tammy with CJ that I think her ass forgot about her own day. Thankfully, today was Saturday, so it wasn't mandatory that she go to the shop.

"I wanna take you to dinner tonight at 8pm," I stated standing at the bathroom door. Janae looked at me through the mirror while still focusing on her hair.

"Okay baby, that's fine. What's the occasion?" she asked, and I just laughed. This girl really forgot her own damn birthday.

"*It's your fucking birthday*," I sang, mocking Drake's song Ratchet Happy Birthday. Janae looked at me for a second and then her mouth flew open.

"Oh shit, it is! How the fuck do I forget my own damn birthday?" she said in a surprised tone. I shook my head at her. "I need to get something to wear. Shit, I'm sitting here doing my hair, I need to be going to get my hair and nails done. Damn, I got so much shit to do now!" she said panicking.

"Chill out man. You about to stress over nothing. I got all that planned out," I said, and she looked at me with a puzzled expression.

"What you mean you have everything figured out?" she asked. I dug in my pocket and handed her a birthday card.

"Read it out loud," I said as she took the card from my hands.

"Nae, it's your motherfucking birthday. How does it feel to be 26? I can't tell you how proud I am to still be your man. I don't want you to worry about shit. Just enjoy your day, starting with going to get your hair and nails done. A car will be waiting for you at 12:30pm. I love you. Happy Birthday," she said and then looked up at me with a big Kool-Aid smile on her face.

She caught me off guard by jumping into my arms and hugging me tight. "Thank you, baby," she said quickly kissing my lips and then going into the bedroom to find something to put on. I smiled knowing that my plan was going smoothly. This shit was going to be one for the books. Although I know she's going to say yes, I'm still nervous as fuck about getting down on one knee.

41

JANAE

"Kai'Juan is really showing the fuck out!" I said excitedly as I walked outside and saw the black 2018 range rover stretch limousine parked outside. I speed walked towards the car and almost peed on myself upon seeing Tammy and baby CJ in the limo.

"Happy Birthday Bitch!" Tammy said excitedly. I smiled as CJ cooed in her arms.

"Thanks boo!" I said reaching out for my nephew. I loved this little boy like he was my own. His curly hair, those light brown eyes and his curly black hair made me fall in love Plus, he just had that newborn baby smell that made me want to have my own child soon. I smiled as I thought about a little Janae or little Kai'Juan running around causing hell. I played with CJ as we drove to Whipped Beauty Bar, my favorite salon to get pampered.

For the next few hours, Tammy and I sat in this shop getting pampered: hair, nails, toes, eyebrows, lashes, make up, everything did. I had my stylist install a frontal with brown highlights. She styled the frontal in a cute half up half down style with curls. I was feeling myself with these 26" bundles in my hair. My make-up was done to perfection as well. I had the make-up artist do a natural beat since I didn't know what the hell I was wearing. Chris came and picked up

CJ from the shop before Tammy and I headed to the mall to find something to wear for the night. I had no idea what we were supposed to be doing, but it was clear that everything was well thought out by Kai'Juan, so I went with the flow.

We arrived at Somerset mall in Troy, MI. I picked out a cute dress that looked almost identical to this dress that I'd seen on Fashion Nova a couple of weeks ago. It was a cold shoulder dress with fringes and a mesh waist which would look good against my milk chocolate skin. I took my phone out to look at a picture of the dress and compare the two. Looking at the picture, I noticed that the title of the dress was Main Attraction, which is exactly what I was going for.

I walked towards the dressing room to try the dress on, and I kept getting a weird feeling that I was being watched. I looked behind me and I could've swore that I saw Lauren standing in the middle of the aisle with a smirk on her face. I blinked a few times and shook my head. Once I opened my eyes again, she was no longer there. I shrugged the feeling off and went on to try on my dress. A few minutes later I came out of the dressing room to show Tammy the dress. The minute she saw me she began snapping her fingers in approval.

"Yaaassss bitch! This dress and that body! You gone be pregnant tonight. Period," she said, and I laughed. Nobody could geek me up like my girl. I went and changed back into my street clothes, paid for my dress and then went to find some shoes. I ended up buying a simple pair of black red bottoms. I didn't want the shoes to take away from the magic of the dress. On the ride back to my house, Tammy decided to go home and get dressed, so I had the driver drop her off. After dropping Tammy off, I headed home. Pulling up to the house, I damn near killed myself trying to hop out of the limo while it was still moving. In my driveway with a big ass bow on it was an all-black 2018 Bugatti Chiron.

"WHAT THE ACTUAL FUCK!" I screamed in excitement as I ran towards the car. Once I got to the car and touched it, I screeched even louder. "No he didn't! No the fuck he didn't!" I ran in the house not even worrying about my bags that were still in the limo. When I opened the front door, I ran straight into Kai'Juan who was casually standing in the foyer.

"You like it?" he asked in a calm and even tone.

"Do I LIKE it? I fucking love it! When the fuck did you...? How? I just...oh my fucking God I'm about to pass out!" I shouted being dramatic. Kai'Juan laughed at me and then dug in his pocket. He handed me the key fob to the car and I jumped up and down excitedly like a kid who'd just received a bike from Santa on Christmas day. "Thank you, baby! Thank you thank you thank you!" I said kissing him repeatedly.

"You ain't gotta thank me. But you do need to hurry up and get dressed before we're late for our reservations," he said.

"Nigga you made reservations? You really showing out today Kai," I said jokingly, and he laughed.

"Just take yo fine ass upstairs and get ready," he said, and I started to go up the stairs, but stopped midstride after remembering that my bags were still in the car. I hurriedly grabbed my bags out of the car and raced back in the house and up the stairs to get dressed.

I took a hoe bath so that I didn't mess up my makeup or hair and proceeded to slip my dress on. About 20 minutes later, I was dressed and walking out of the bathroom. Kai'Juan was finishing getting ready with his back towards me. I don't even know what exactly he had on, but he looked good as hell from the back.

"How do I look baby?" I asked, and he turned around upon hearing my voice. Kai'Juan gave me the once over and then licked his lips like I was gravy and he was a biscuit.

"If you ain't with me, you ain't wearing that dress," he said, and I rolled my eyes playfully.

"Ok so that means I'm a bad bitch," I said and laughed.

"Hell yeah that's what that means. I'm serious. Wear that shit while you not with me and see what happens," he said as he slapped my ass as I walked past.

"You looking like a meal yourself Mr. Sears," I said eyeing my man. He had on a black button up with black slacks and black studded red bottoms on his feet. "I started to buy heels similar to your shoes earlier, but I thought it would take away from the dress," I stated, and he gave me a smirk before going into his closet. He reappeared with a Christian Louboutin box and handed it to me. I went and sat on the bed before opening the box. Opening it, I saw the same pair of studded red bottoms that I saw in the store earlier and I looked up at Kai'Juan who was cheesing. He was eating this shit up.

"Now how the hell did you know I wanted these?" I asked him.

"A little birdy told me," he said still cheesing.

"Tammy," I said and we both laughed. That's why I fucked with T.

"You full of surprises today huh?" I asked, and he bent down to kiss my lips.

"You have no idea."

42

KAI'JUAN

*W*alking into Ruth Chris, I was nervous as fuck. A nigga like me was really about to turn his playa card in. I'm still shocked. Out of nervousness, I kept fidgeting with the ring box in my pocket. Janae was too busy running her mouth with Tammy to notice that I was sweating bullets.

"You good?" Chris asked, whispering in my ear.

"Hell nah. I wanna just get this shit over with now," I told him, and he laughed. Just wait until this nigga decided to propose to Tammy, I was gonna roast his ass every fucking chance I got. Bitch ass nigga.

A server led us to the private room that I'd booked for dinner. To Janae's surprise, I flew her Mom in from Florida. She just retired last year and she's in Florida living her best life with all the other old retired folk. As soon as Janae entered the room she burst out into tears. Her Mom stood up to hug her and wish her a happy birthday.

After the initial shock of her Mom being here wore off, we ordered our food and had a nice casual dinner. I know she wished her Dad could be here, but he was only a phone call away. A nigga had some pull, but I can't be getting mothafuckas out of jail and shit.

While we were finishing up dinner, I excused myself to the bathroom, but I was really going to let the staff know that I was ready. I stopped at the bathroom briefly and splashed some water on my face. I ain't never been this fucking nervous. Not even in court.

I walked back into the private room and the sever that I had waiting looked at me for his que. I nodded and then the lights in the room grew dim. Suddenly, Ja Rule and Lil Mo's *Put It on Me* began to play. Janae busted out laughing as soon as it started. When we were younger, she loved this fucking song and said that if she ever got married she'd want this song played at her wedding. A slideshow began to play with pictures of Janae and I throughout our relationship. I'd been with this girl, off and on for the past 6 years, so seeing some of these old ass pictures from when we first started made me feel a way. I heard a bunch of awes and laughs coming from everyone in the room as they watched the slideshow. Janae's eyes were plastered to the screen. I could tell that she was loving it.

As the song ended, I grabbed her hand and had her stand up. The lights came back on and I proceeded to make my announcement.

"I just want to thank y'all for coming to help celebrate my baby's 26th birthday. I know that you all," I said looking at Janae's mom "haven't been too fond of me over the years, and I take complete responsibility for all the things that I've done, and I hope that you can forgive me," I said to them.

Janae's mom nodded her head and in approval. "You were forgiven a long time ago Kai'Juan," she said, and I nodded my head as well.

"Janae, I just want to say that I love you and I know that I treated you like shit for a long time. Through all of that, you stayed right by my side, no matter what anybody says. You love me unconditionally, gave me loyalty and stability and I can't tell you how much that means to me. When all these bitches wanted was dick and money, excuse my French y'all, you just wanted me. You are my heart, my backbone, my rib," I said mocking Kevin Hart. "It took me a while to grow the fuck up and realize what was really important. Baby, as long as I got you, I know that my life is fucking lit. I don't want to leave this world and feel like I failed you. I want to spend the rest of my life loving you the right way and creating a legacy, a family with you. With that being said..." I said getting down on one knee. "Janae Renae Evans, will you marry me?" I asked. I looked in her eyes and saw the tears coming down her face. She smiled through her tears and just looked at me for a few moments. I started to get nervous thinking that she would turn a nigga down.

"Girl say something!" Tammy said, and everyone laughed.

"Yes baby, I'll marry you!" she said, and I slipped the ring on her finger. "This shit is huge!" she said, and once again, everybody laughed. I stood up and kissed and hugged her. Everyone congratulated us, and we sat back down to eat dessert and then get out of here.

"Issa fiancé!" Janae said taking a snapchat video of her ring. I just laughed and shook my head.

43

JANAE

I can't believe this man! All in one day, I received a car and a proposal. I don't think he can top himself next year. I'm still in shock. Then, to bring my mom here was really the icing on the cake. She fucking hated Kai'Juan because of the shit he was doing to me, but I was so sure that he would get it together, and my baby did.

After eating the delicious strawberry cheesecake, I let Kai'Juan know that I had to use the restroom. Tammy offered to go with me, but I told her I was good to go by myself since it was right next to the private room. I went to the restroom, handled my business and then headed back towards the private room. Just like earlier, I had this eerie feeling that I was being watched. I turned around to see if there was anyone behind me or staring at me, but I didn't see anyone. I turned back around and entered the private room where everyone was preparing to leave. My mom came up to me and kissed me on the cheek.

"Congratulations sweetheart. I'm so proud of you! I'll be in town for the next few days, so make sure that we at least have lunch or dinner together," she said, and I promised her that we would. After saying goodbye to my her, Chris, Tammy, CJ, Kai'Juan and I walked out of the restaurant and climbed in the limo to leave.

"So what you tryna do now fiancé?" Kai'Juan asked and I smiled. I'll never get tired of hearing that.

"It's a celebration so we're going to the club. Are the parents coming or y'all too old to hang with us childless adults?" I said jokingly, and Tammy stuck up her middle finger.

"You can go if you want T but I'm tired as fuck. I'mma head home with CJ" Chris said, and I frowned.

"No nigga, you coming with her or ain't neither one of y'all coming. You just gone let her go to the club by herself?" I said with a little attitude.

"She ain't by herself, she with y'all," Chris replied. Tammy looked like she wanted to slap the shit out of him, but didn't say shit. That quick, the energy in the limo was tense. I may have been being a brat, but I felt like Chris should go if not for the simple fact that it's my birthday AND I just got engaged, at least to have some fun with your girl. According to Tammy, they haven't been out or had sex since CJ was born and Tammy's six weeks was up two weeks ago. I rolled my eyes and folded my arms under my breasts.

Kai'Juan wrapped his arm around me and pulled me closer to him. He kissed my cheek and then told me not to let Chris fuck up our night.

"You good bae, you with me don't even tri...."

SKKKKKRRRRRRRRTTTTTT!!! BOOM!

Kai'Juan was cut off by the loud sound of tires screeching. The limo started to swerve uncontrollably, and Tammy and I screamed before we felt the limo crash into another car.

TO BE CONTINUED...